Delegated Investing and Optimal Risk Budgets

Dissertation

zur Erlangung des Grades

eines Doktors der

wirtschaftlichen Staatswissenschaften

(Dr. rer. pol.)

des Fachbereichs Rechts- und

Wirtschaftswissenschaften

der

Johannes Gutenberg-Universität Mainz

vorgelegt von

Dipl.-Math. oec. Markus O. Starck, M.S. (USA)

Wissenschaftlicher Mitarbeiter in Mainz

2007

Erstberichterstatter:	Prof. Dr. Siegfried Trautmann
Zweitberichterstatter:	Prof. Dr. Dietmar Leisen
Tag der mündlichen Prüfung:	25. Oktober 2007

Schriftenreihe

Finanzmanagement

Band 49

ISSN 1439-5266

Verlag Dr. Kovač

Markus O. Starck

Delegated Investing and Optimal Risk Budgets

Verlag Dr. Kovač

Hamburg
2008

Leverkusenstr. 13 · 22761 Hamburg · Tel. 040 - 39 88 80-0 · Fax 040 - 39 88 80-55

E-Mail info@verlagdrkovac.de · Internet www.verlagdrkovac.de

Dissertation des Fachbereichs Rechts- und Wirtschaftswissenschaften der Johannes Gutenberg-Universität Mainz.

Erstberichterstatter: Prof. Dr. Siegfried Trautmann
Zweitberichterstatter: Prof. Dr. Dietmar Leisen
Tag der mündlichen Prüfung: 25. Oktober 2007

Bibliografische Information der Deutschen Nationalbibliothek
Die Deutsche Nationalbibliothek verzeichnet diese Publikation in der Deutschen Nationalbibliografie; detaillierte bibliografische Daten sind im Internet über http://dnb.d-nb.de abrufbar.

ISSN: 1439-5266

ISBN: 978-3-8300-3612-8

Zugl.: Dissertation, Universität Mainz, 2007

Umschlaggestaltung: VDK

Printed in Germany

Gedruckt auf holz-, chlor- und säurefreiem Papier Alster Digital. Alster Digital ist alterungsbeständig und erfüllt die Normen für Archivbeständigkeit ANSI 3948 und ISO 9706.

Preface

The research presented in this dissertation was conducted at the CoFaR Center of Finance and Risk Management at the Johannes Gutenberg University of Mainz, Germany. I gratefully acknowledge the sponsorship of the CoFaR by the Aareal Bank AG, the LRP Landesbank Rheinland-Pfalz, and the Ministerium für Bildung, Wissenschaft, Jugend und Kultur of the federal state Rheinland-Pfalz.

First of all, I want to thank my supervisor Prof. Dr. Siegfried Trautmann for his support and advice as well as for providing an intellectually stimulating work environment. The idea to analyze delegation problems raised while preparing the tutorials for Professor Trautmann's advanced lectures in finance. I appreciate the opportunity to additionally research in the field of credit risk and want to thank Professor Trautmann for coauthoring an article on reduced form credit risk models. I would like to thank Prof. Dr. Dietmar Leisen for agreeing to be the secondary advisor. I want to thank former and current colleagues Monika Müller, Manuel Gauer, Daniel Lange, Tobias Linder, Tin-Kwai Man, and Dr. Marco Schulmerich for helpful discussions. Together with Marita Lehn, they have created a pleasant and supportive work environment.

I would like to express my appreciation for the continuous support of my parents Anneliese and Elmar Starck. Finally, I want to thank my wife Christina Tank for her love and support all the way.

Markus O. Starck

Contents

List of Figures

List of Tables

Symbols

$\boldsymbol{A}$	information matrix of frontier portfolios
a, b, c	elements of information matrix $\boldsymbol{A}$
d	frontier portfolios' ratio of squared relative return and relative risk with reference portfolio MVP
f	management fee
B	benchmark portfolio
G	gain
$\boldsymbol{H}$	generalized information matrix
K	constant used in relationship of expected return and beta
m_p	slope of shortfall line with shortfall probability p
P	portfolio with expected return μ_P and volatility σ_P
P^*	frontier portfolio with expected return $\mu_{P^*} = \mu_P$
$\widehat{P}$	efficient frontier portfolio with volatility $\sigma_{P^*} = \sigma_P$
Q	portfolio with maximum mean-volatility ratio
R_j, R_P	return of jth asset, return of portfolio P
$\boldsymbol{s}$	composition of shifting strategy
$\boldsymbol{V}$	covariance matrix of asset returns
$\mathbf{x}_P$	composition of portfolio P measured as relative weights in assets
$\beta_{j,P}$	beta of asset j measured with respect to portfolio P
$\boldsymbol{\beta}_{\vert P}$	vector of betas of all assets measured with respect to portfolio P
μ_j, μ_P	expected return of asset j, expected return of portfolio P

μ_s	expected excess return of shifting strategy
$\boldsymbol{\mu}$	vector of expected asset returns
$\sigma_{i,j}$	covariance of asset returns R_i and R_j
σ_P, σ_s	standard deviation of portfolio return and of excess return of shifting strategy
$\boldsymbol{\sigma}_s$	vector of tracking errors
τ	threshold return
Φ	standard normal cumulative distribution function
$\mathbf{0}$	vector with each element being 0
$\mathbf{1}$	vector with each element being 1
$\boldsymbol{A}'$	transposition of a matrix $\boldsymbol{A}$
$\frac{\partial f}{\partial \mathbf{x}}$	vector of partial derivatives $\left(\frac{\partial f}{\partial x_1}, \ldots, \frac{\partial f}{\partial x_n}\right)'$

List of Abbreviations

et al.	et alii (and others)
i.e.	id est (that is)
et seq.	et sequentes or et sequentia (and the following)
KAG	Kapitalanlagegesellschaft (investment company)
KAGG	Gesetz über Kapitalanlagegesellschaften (Act on Investment Companies)
MSCI	Morgan Stanley Capital International
MVP	minimum variance portfolio
p.	page
pp.	pages
USD	United States Dollar
TEV	tracking error volatility
TEVBR	tracking error volatility and beta restriction
VaR	Value at Risk

Chapter 1

Introduction

The theory of investment has to address the fact that investment decisions on the majority of wealth are delegated to financial professionals. Outsourcing and delegating investment authority has gained attention recently specifically by investment companies. German investment companies are allowed to outsource investment advisory responsibilities to third parties by the amendment of the Act on Investment Companies.[1] In order to investigate the investment process of delegating financial decisions, insights offered by portfolio theory and principal-agent theory need to be integrated into a comprehensive theory of delegated investing. The scientific exploration of this field and its implications on asset pricing is identified to be the "next frontier" of research, as noted by Allen (2001) and Ambachtsheer (2005).

Cornell and Roll (2005) present an asset pricing model with delegating investors and conclude that, when all decisions are delegated, asset pricing depends on objective functions of institutional investors, not on utility functions of individuals. We advance their approach by arguing that in-

[1]On March 20, 2002, the German government passed the amendment of the Act on Investment Companies ("viertes Finanzmarktförderungsgesetz") that allows investors to outsource discretionary investment advisory responsibilities to third parties such as Master KAGs ("Kapitalanlagegesellschaften"). See also page 106.

vestors do have instruments to control the agents. Although investors may be less informed about the financial market, they can control their agents by setting risk limits. The institutional implementation of this kind of control are departments for financial controlling and risk management. Their purpose is to prevent severe losses and to control financial risks and success via given risk limits and return targets. This dissertation presents models of risk controling delegated investment decisions and studies implications on asset pricing.

The proposed investment theory integrates principal-agent issues into portfolio theory. In our model framework, investors delegate portfolio selection to portfolio managers due to lack of information. The investor can define a strategic benchmark portfolio according to the investment objective and improve it by adding active management. The active management's flexibility in deviating from the benchmark can be controlled via the size of tracking error constraints. Roll (1992) derives the agent's benchmark-relative portfolio selection in the presence of tracking error constraints. We show how to set the constraints optimally such that the delegated relative portfolio selection is optimal for the overall absolute objective.

The analysis may be specifically useful for the management of funds as one of the investigated objectives is minimizing the probability of the portfolio return falling short a fixed target return. This was introduced as "safety first" approach by Roy (1952). Benchmark orientation and shortfall minimization is e.g. relevant for pension funds that guarantee a minimum return as well as participation in benchmark performance. Furthermore, we also study the optimal active risk allocation when the principal's objective is to minimize the delegated portfolio's Value at Risk. An optimal active risk allocation for the delegated investment decisions ensures that the extend of active management that is added to the benchmark allocation is chosen optimally for the overall absolute objective. We further investigate whether it is possible to separate asset allocation and active risk allocation in delegated portfolio management.

The contributions to the literature are on following fields of the theory of investing:

- Information theory: The models are able to explain that investors delegate investment decisions to professionals due to lack of information. They show which financial information is necessary in order to control the agent's portfolio selection with constraints. Type and value of portfolio constraints are chosen depending on the principal's level of information.

- Principal-agent theory: The models incorporate typical principal-agent relationships of the investment process. Investors decide on the optimal risk allocation in order to give the right amount of flexibility to the delegated investment decisions and to induce the agents to select portfolios on their behalf.

- Portfolio theory: We integrate benchmark oriented investing and shortfall-risk based objectives. Closed form solutions are given for the optimal amount of active risk, e.g. to implement the safety first approach in delegated investing or to minimize the portfolio's Value at Risk.

- Governance of funds: We study the impact of the chosen type of constraints on portfolio selection and resulting performance. The models represent possible organizational set-ups of delegating investment authority.

Chapters 2 and 3 review classical results of portfolio theory concerning the mean-variance frontier and results of portfolio selection when a benchmark is given. Chapter 4 contributes to the literature by combining benchmark oriented investing and the safety first approach: The investor delegates portfolio selection to a benchmark outperforming portfolio manager and uses benchmark tracking constraints for minimizing the probability of the delegated portfolio falling short a target return. Chapter 5 derives optimal constraints for a delegating investor who aims at minimizing the portfolio's Value at Risk. Chapter 6 studies implications of delegated investing on market equilibrium when all delegating investors minimize shortfall risk. Figure 1.1 shows the structure of the model development so far. In addition, chapter 7 studies the simultaneous strategic asset and risk allocation when investment decisions are delegated to multiple agents.

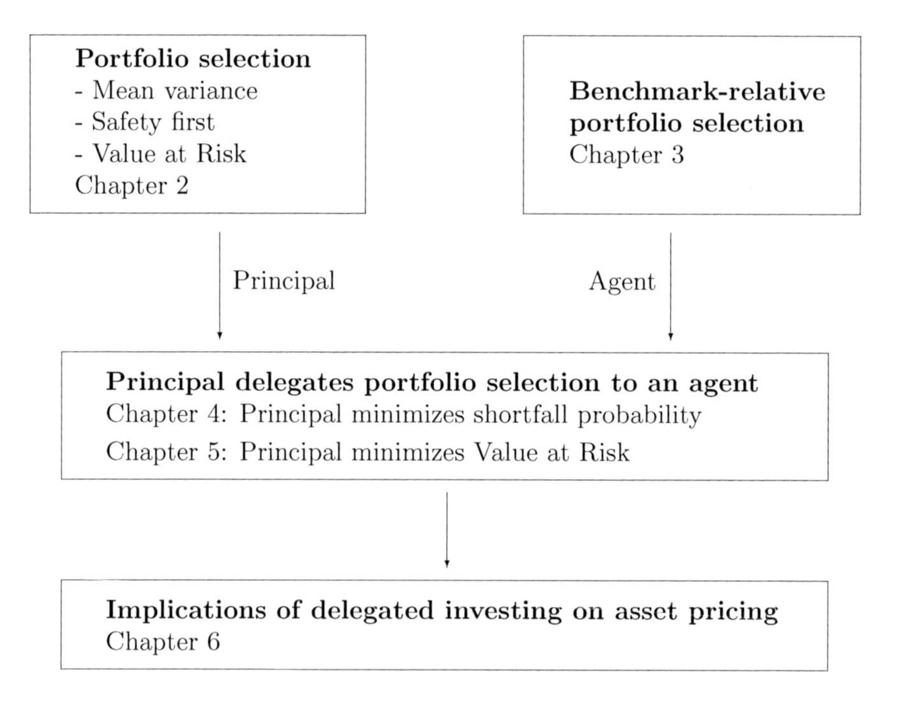

Figure 1.1: Outline of the Model Presentation in Chapters 2 – 6

Chapter 2

Portfolio Selection

This chapter provides a comprehensive review of classical results of portfolio theory. The essential topic of portfolio theory is the allocation of investments in assets such that the relationship of risk and return is optimized. This chapter presents central ideas and derives key results for the optimal portfolio selection. These classical models are the basis for developing models of delegated investing in subsequent chapters.

Portfolios with minimum risk for a given expected return characterize the risk-return relationship of the optimal combination of investment opportunities. A central element of the presentation of this chapter is the information matrix which can be used to describe the relationship of expected return and variance of portfolios with minimum risk. The information matrix is the key tool for deriving the optimal portfolio selection based on risk measures such as the variance of return or the probability of missing a target return.

Section 2.1 provides an introduction and overview of standard problems of portfolio theory. Since most results are well known in literature, this section already provides references to the solutions which the interested reader finds fully elaborated in the subsequent sections. Sections 2.2 – 2.4 study optimal portfolios of exclusively risky assets based on the risk measures variance and shortfall probability. A riskless asset is added in section 2.5 where optimal portfolios with minimum variance are derived. The last section 2.6 studies optimal asset allocations for each model based on historical data of national indices.

2.1 Introduction to Portfolio Selection

Portfolio theory is concerned with the relationship of risk and return when investment opportunities are combined. A typical task is determining optimal portfolios according to a given objective such as minimizing the variance of return. This section introduces the reader to classical portfolio selection problems. The basic model assumptions of portfolio theory are:

Assumption 2.1 (Frictionless Market).
There are no market frictions such as transaction costs, taxes, shortsale constraints and assets are divisible.

Assumption 2.2 (Risky Assets).
There are n risky assets that are traded in the market and no riskless asset is available. The asset returns R_i, $i = 1, \ldots, n$, have expected returns $\boldsymbol{\mu} = (\mu_1, \ldots, \mu_n)'$ and positive definite covariance matrix $\boldsymbol{V} \equiv (\sigma_{i,j})_{i,j=1,\ldots,n}$, where $\sigma_{i,j} \equiv Cov(R_i, R_j)$. There are at least two assets with distinct expected returns.

Assumption 2.3 (Mean-Variance Criterion).
The investor chooses portfolios based on the mean-variance criterion: Portfolio P_1 is preferred to portfolio P_2 according to the mean-variance criterion if and only if

a) $\mu_{P_1} \geq \mu_{P_2}$ and $\sigma_{P_1} < \sigma_{P_2}$

or b) $\mu_{P_1} > \mu_{P_2}$ and $\sigma_{P_1} \leq \sigma_{P_2}$.

A portfolio P is *efficient* if there does not exist a portfolio that is preferred to P according to the mean-variance criterion. Markowitz (1952) explores the problem of an investor who wants to earn a certain expected return and diversify the risks of the investments. More formally, the investor wants to compose a portfolio $\mathbf{x}_P = (x_1, \ldots, x_n)'$ that minimizes the risk measured by the variance of the return, $\sigma_P^2 = \mathbf{x}_P' \boldsymbol{V} \mathbf{x}_P = \sum_{i=1}^n \sum_{j=1}^n x_i x_j \sigma_{i,j}$, for a given level of expected return $\mu_P = \mathbf{x}_P' \boldsymbol{\mu} = \sum_{i=1}^n x_i \mu_i$, where x_i denotes the proportion of total wealth invested in the ith asset. This problem is known as the standard problem of portfolio theory.

Problem 2.1 (Minimize Variance Given Expected Portfolio Return). *Determine the optimal portfolio composition such that the variance of the portfolio return is minimized for a given expected portfolio return:*

$$
\begin{aligned}
\textit{objective:} \quad & \min_{\mathbf{x}_P} \sigma_P^2 \\
\textit{constraints:} \quad & \mathbf{x}_P' \boldsymbol{\mu} = \mu_P \\
& \mathbf{x}_P' \mathbf{1} = 1 \quad .
\end{aligned}
$$

The solution of this problem is called *frontier portfolio* or *minimum variance portfolio at a given expected return level.* The *(mean-variance) frontier* is the set of frontier portfolios of all levels of expected returns. The frontier can also be defined as the set of portfolios that maximize or minimize the expected return for all levels of total risk. The problem of maximizing expected returns reads:

Problem 2.2 (Maximize Expected Return Given Total Portfolio Risk). *Determine the optimal portfolio composition such that the expected return is maximized for a given level of total risk:*

$$
\begin{aligned}
\textit{objective:} \quad & \max_{\mathbf{x}_P} \mu_P \\
\textit{constraints:} \quad & \mathbf{x}_P' \boldsymbol{V} \mathbf{x}_P = \sigma_P^2 \\
& \mathbf{x}_P' \mathbf{1} = 1 \quad .
\end{aligned}
$$

Table 2.1: Classical Portfolio Selection Problems

Portfolio selection problem and author	Objective function and constraints	Solution and expected portfolio return
Minimize variance	$\min_{\mathbf{x}_P} \mathbf{x}_P' \boldsymbol{V} \mathbf{x}_P$	$\mathbf{x}_P = \boldsymbol{V}^{-1}(\boldsymbol{\mu}\ \mathbf{1})\boldsymbol{A}^{-1}\begin{pmatrix} \mu_P \\ 1 \end{pmatrix}$
given expected return	$\boldsymbol{\mu}'\mathbf{x}_P = \mu_P$	proposition 2.3
Markowitz (1952)	$\mathbf{x}_P'\mathbf{1} = 1$	
Maximize expected return	$\max_{\mathbf{x}_P} \mathbf{x}_P' \boldsymbol{\mu}$	$\mu_P = \mu_{\mathrm{MVP}} + \sqrt{d}\sqrt{\sigma_P^2 - \sigma_{\mathrm{MVP}}^2}$
given variance	$\mathbf{x}_P' \boldsymbol{V} \mathbf{x}_P = \sigma_P^2$	equation (2.12)
	$\mathbf{x}_P'\mathbf{1} = 1$	
Safety first approach	$\min_{\mathbf{x}_P} P(R_P < \tau)$	$\mu_P = \frac{a-b\tau}{b-c\tau}$
Roy (1952)	$\mathbf{x}_P'\mathbf{1} = 1$	proposition 2.6
Maximize threshold return	$\max_{\mathbf{x}_P} \tau$	$\tau = \mu_{\mathrm{MVP}} - \sqrt{m_p^2 - d}\ \sigma_{\mathrm{MVP}}$
Kataoka (1963)	$P(R_P < \tau) = \mathrm{p}$	$\mu_P = \mu_{\mathrm{MVP}} + \frac{d\sigma_{\mathrm{MVP}}}{\sqrt{m_p^2 - d}}$
		proposition 2.8
Maximize expected return	$\max_{\mathbf{x}_P} \mu_P$	proposition 2.10
given a threshold return	$P(R_P < \tau) = \mathrm{p}$	
and a shortfall probability		
Telser (1955)		

This table provides an overview on classical portfolio selection problems and their solutions. Since the optimal portfolio of each problem is on the mean-variance frontier, the optimal composition can be calculated with equation (2.1) below and the expected portfolio return given in the third column of the table.

There are many variants of these problems with further restrictions. A typical restriction in practical portfolio construction is the exclusion of shortsale, $x_i \geq 0$, $i = 1, \ldots, n$, since shortsale of assets is expensive and often prohibited by financial regulation rules or portfolio policies. Since closed form solutions often only exist in case of absence of complex restrictions, we do not consider such restrictions in the following. Other classical objective functions for portfolio selection are e.g. minimizing the probability of falling short a target return or maximizing the target return given a shortfall probability. The solution of these problems are also on the efficient frontier. Table 2.1 provides an overview on classical portfolio optimization problems and their solutions that are derived in the subsequent sections.

2.2 The Efficient Frontier without a Riskless Asset

This section derives the solution for the classical portfolio selection problems 2.1 and 2.2 and introduces the information matrix. Most results are due to Markowitz (1952), Merton (1972), and Roll (1977). A readable introduction can be found in Trautmann (2007, chapter 5).

The (efficient set) *information matrix* $\boldsymbol{A}$ simplifies the representation of optimal portfolios. It is defined by

$$\boldsymbol{A} \equiv \begin{pmatrix} a & b \\ b & c \end{pmatrix} \equiv (\boldsymbol{\mu} \;\; \mathbf{1})' \boldsymbol{V}^{-1} (\boldsymbol{\mu} \;\; \mathbf{1}) \, ,$$

where notation is introduced for the n-dimensional vector $\mathbf{1} \equiv (1 \;\; 1 \;\; \ldots \;\; 1)'$ and for the elements $a \equiv \boldsymbol{\mu}' \boldsymbol{V}^{-1} \boldsymbol{\mu}$, $b \equiv \mathbf{1}' \boldsymbol{V}^{-1} \boldsymbol{\mu}$, and $c \equiv \mathbf{1}' \boldsymbol{V}^{-1} \mathbf{1}$ of the information matrix.[1]

[1]Please note that we use the vector notation of Roll (1977, appendix) which is slightly different from the one in Merton (1972). Readers used to Merton's notation know the elements of the information matrix as $A \widehat{=} b$, $B \widehat{=} a$, and $C \widehat{=} c$.

Proposition 2.3 (Frontier Portfolios).
The solution of the variance minimization problem 2.1 for given expected return μ_P is a frontier portfolio P with composition

$$\mathbf{x}_P = \boldsymbol{V}^{-1}(\boldsymbol{\mu}\ \mathbf{1})\boldsymbol{A}^{-1}\begin{pmatrix}\mu_P\\ 1\end{pmatrix} \tag{2.1}$$

and variance

$$\sigma_P^2 = (\mu_P\ 1)\boldsymbol{A}^{-1}\begin{pmatrix}\mu_P\\ 1\end{pmatrix} = \frac{a - 2b\mu_P + c\mu_P^2}{ac - b^2}\,. \tag{2.2}$$

Proof. We first show that the information matrix is regular. The rank of the vector $(\boldsymbol{\mu}\ \mathbf{1})$ is two according to assumption 2.2. Then, the vector $\boldsymbol{u} = (\boldsymbol{\mu}\ \mathbf{1})\boldsymbol{v}$ is different from zero for each $\boldsymbol{v} \neq (0 \quad 0)'$ and

$$\boldsymbol{v}'\boldsymbol{A}^{-1}\boldsymbol{v} = \boldsymbol{v}'(\boldsymbol{\mu}\ \mathbf{1})'\boldsymbol{V}^{-1}(\boldsymbol{\mu}\ \mathbf{1})\boldsymbol{v} = \boldsymbol{u}'\boldsymbol{V}^{-1}\boldsymbol{u} > 0\,,$$

since $\boldsymbol{V}$ and its inverse $\boldsymbol{V}^{-1}$ are positive definite. This equation is equivalent to $\boldsymbol{A}$ being regular.

The chapter's appendix discusses conditions for the optimal solution of an optimization problem. Problem 2.1 can be solved with the method of Lagrange multipliers. The Lagrange function reads

$$L(\mathbf{x}, \boldsymbol{\lambda}) = \mathbf{x}'\boldsymbol{V}\mathbf{x} + \lambda_1(\mu_P - \mathbf{x}'\boldsymbol{\mu}) + \lambda_2(1 - \mathbf{x}'\mathbf{1})\,.$$

Since $\boldsymbol{V}$ is positive definite, the optimal solution $\mathbf{x}^*$ is unique, has minimum variance at the given expected return level μ_P, and satisfies the conditions

$$\frac{\partial L}{\partial \mathbf{x}}(\mathbf{x}^*, \boldsymbol{\lambda}^*) = 2\boldsymbol{V}\mathbf{x}^* - \lambda_1^*\boldsymbol{\mu} - \lambda_2^*\mathbf{1} = \mathbf{0} \tag{2.3}$$

$$\frac{\partial L}{\partial \lambda_1}(\mathbf{x}^*, \boldsymbol{\lambda}^*) = \mu_P - \mathbf{x}^{*\prime}\boldsymbol{\mu} = 0 \tag{2.4}$$

$$\frac{\partial L}{\partial \lambda_2}(\mathbf{x}^*, \boldsymbol{\lambda}^*) = 1 - \mathbf{x}^{*\prime}\mathbf{1} = 0\,. \tag{2.5}$$

Since $\boldsymbol{V}$ is regular, solving equation (2.3) for $\mathbf{x}^*$ yields:

$$\mathbf{x}^* = \frac{1}{2}\boldsymbol{V}^{-1}(\boldsymbol{\mu}\ \mathbf{1})\begin{pmatrix}\lambda_1^* \\ \lambda_2^*\end{pmatrix}. \tag{2.6}$$

Multiplying with $(\boldsymbol{\mu}\ \mathbf{1})'$ results in:

$$\begin{pmatrix}\boldsymbol{\mu}' \\ \mathbf{1}'\end{pmatrix}\mathbf{x}^* = \frac{1}{2}\begin{pmatrix}\boldsymbol{\mu}' \\ \mathbf{1}'\end{pmatrix}\boldsymbol{V}^{-1}(\boldsymbol{\mu}\ \mathbf{1})\begin{pmatrix}\lambda_1^* \\ \lambda_2^*\end{pmatrix} = \frac{1}{2}\boldsymbol{A}\begin{pmatrix}\lambda_1^* \\ \lambda_2^*\end{pmatrix}.$$

Since $\boldsymbol{A}$ is regular, multiplying with $2\boldsymbol{A}^{-1}$ and using equations (2.4) and (2.5) provides the optimal Lagrange multipliers

$$2\boldsymbol{A}^{-1}\begin{pmatrix}\mu_P \\ 1\end{pmatrix} = 2\boldsymbol{A}^{-1}\begin{pmatrix}\boldsymbol{\mu}' \\ \mathbf{1}'\end{pmatrix}\mathbf{x}^* = \begin{pmatrix}\lambda_1^* \\ \lambda_2^*\end{pmatrix}$$

which yields the optimal composition with equation (2.6). The variance follows directly from $\sigma_P^2 = \mathbf{x}^{*\prime}\boldsymbol{V}\mathbf{x}^*$, equation (2.1), symmetry $\boldsymbol{V}' = \boldsymbol{V}$, and the definition of the information matrix.

As a final remark, we note that the optimal Lagrange multipliers are

$$\begin{aligned}\begin{pmatrix}\lambda_1^* \\ \lambda_2^*\end{pmatrix} &= 2\boldsymbol{A}^{-1}\begin{pmatrix}\mu_P \\ 1\end{pmatrix} = \frac{2}{ac-b^2}\begin{pmatrix}c & -b \\ -b & a\end{pmatrix}\begin{pmatrix}\mu_P \\ 1\end{pmatrix} \\ &= \frac{2}{a-\frac{b^2}{c}}\begin{pmatrix}\mu_P - \frac{b}{c} \\ \frac{a}{c} - \frac{b}{c}\mu_P\end{pmatrix}\end{aligned}$$

and that the multiplier λ_1^* can be seen as the marginal increment of variance with respect to the expected return: $\frac{\partial\sigma_P^2}{\partial\mu_P} \stackrel{(2.2)}{=} \frac{2}{a-\frac{b^2}{c}}\left(\mu_P - \frac{b}{c}\right) = \lambda_1^*$. □

Reducing portfolio risk is a central topic of portfolio theory. The portfolio with least variance of return is called the minimum variance portfolio (MVP). The MVP has expected return, variance, and composition

$$\mu_{\text{MVP}} = \frac{b}{c} \tag{2.7}$$

$$\sigma_{\text{MVP}}^2 = \frac{1}{c} \tag{2.8}$$

$$\mathbf{x}_{\text{MVP}} = \frac{1}{c}\boldsymbol{V}^{-1}\mathbf{1}$$

which can be derived using the condition $\partial\sigma_P^2/\partial\mu_P = 0$ and equations (2.2) and (2.1). Rearranging equation (2.2) shows that all frontier portfolios different from MVP have an identical ratio of squared relative return and relative total risk

$$d \equiv \frac{(\mu_P - \mu_{\text{MVP}})^2}{\sigma_P^2 - \sigma_{\text{MVP}}^2} = \frac{\left(\mu_P - \frac{b}{c}\right)^2}{\sigma_P^2 - \frac{1}{c}} = a - \frac{b^2}{c} \tag{2.9}$$

with MVP as reference portfolio.

Rearranging this equation shows that frontier portfolios are located on a hyperbola in (μ, σ)-space with center $(\mu_{\text{MVP}}, 0)$, as is also illustrated in figure 2.1. The hyperbola equation reads

$$\frac{\sigma_P^2}{\sigma_{\text{MVP}}^2} - \frac{(\mu_P - \mu_{\text{MVP}})^2}{d\sigma_{\text{MVP}}^2} = 1 \tag{2.10}$$

with slope $\pm\sqrt{d}$ of the asymptotes.

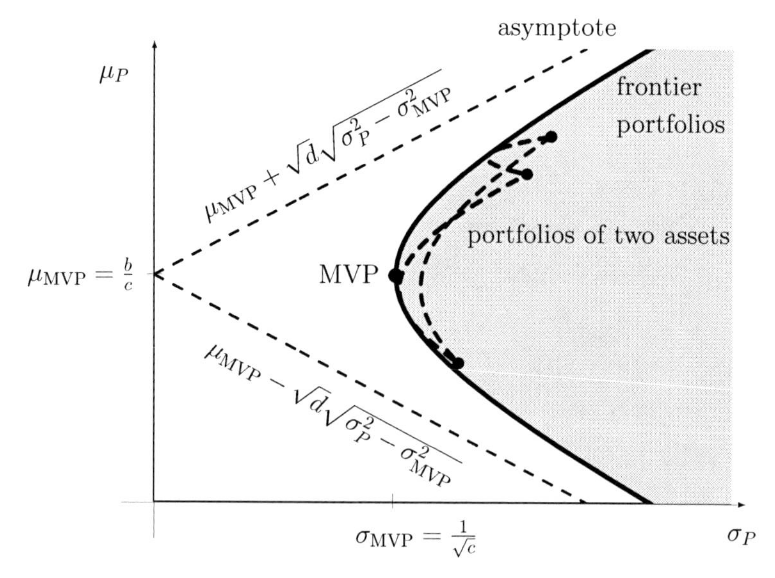

Figure 2.1: Frontier Portfolios are Located on a Hyperbola in (μ, σ)-Space

Figure 2.2 illustrates that frontier portfolios have identical ratio d. Then, the total risk of frontier portfolios simplifies to

$$\sigma_P^2 = \sigma_{\text{MVP}}^2 + \frac{(\mu_P - \mu_{\text{MVP}})^2}{d} . \tag{2.11}$$

The expected return of a frontier portfolio with total risk σ_P^2 is

$$\mu_P = \mu_{\text{MVP}} \pm \sqrt{d}\sqrt{\sigma_P^2 - \sigma_{\text{MVP}}^2} , \tag{2.12}$$

where the plus and the minus signs correspond to an efficient and to an inefficient frontier portfolio, respectively.

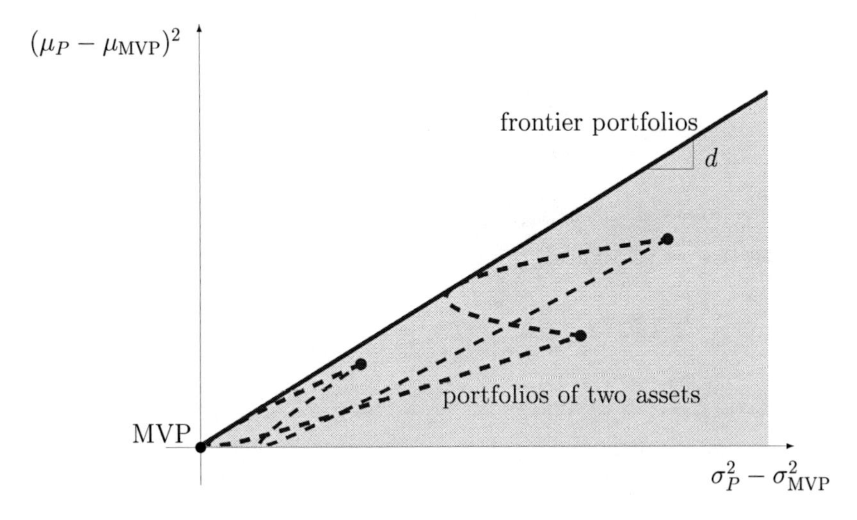

Figure 2.2: Frontier Portfolios have Identical Ratio $d = \frac{(\mu_P - \mu_{\text{MVP}})^2}{\sigma_P^2 - \sigma_{\text{MVP}}^2}$

Frontier portfolios with zero correlation and tangent portfolios are closely related and also important in portfolio theory. The returns R_{P_1}, R_{P_2} of two frontier portfolios P_1 and P_2 have covariance

$$\sigma_{P_1,P_2} = (\mu_{P_1}\ 1)\boldsymbol{A}^{-1}\begin{pmatrix}\mu_{P_2}\\ 1\end{pmatrix} = \frac{a - b\mu_{P_1} - b\mu_{P_2} + c\mu_{P_1}\mu_{P_2}}{ac - b^2} \tag{2.13}$$

which follows from $\sigma_{P_1,P_2} = \mathbf{x}'_{P_1}\boldsymbol{V}\mathbf{x}_{P_2}$ and equation (2.1). Two portfolios P and Z are called *orthogonal* if the covariance of their returns vanishes: $\sigma_{P,Z} = 0$. Given a frontier portfolio P with expected return μ_P, $\mu_P \neq \mu_{\text{MVP}}$, the expected return and variance of the orthogonal frontier portfolio follow from equations (2.13) and (2.2):

$$\mu_Z = \frac{a - b\mu_P}{b - c\mu_P} \tag{2.14}$$

$$\sigma_Z^2 = \frac{a - 2b\mu_P + c\mu_P^2}{(b - c\mu_P)^2}\,. \tag{2.15}$$

Given a tangency point T on the hyperbola, a point P on the tangent fulfills[2]

$$\frac{\sigma_T\,\sigma_P}{\sigma_{\text{MVP}}^2} - \frac{(\mu_T - \mu_{\text{MVP}})(\mu_P - \mu_{\text{MVP}})}{d\,\sigma_{\text{MVP}}^2} = 1\,.$$

Since the point $(\mu_P, \sigma_P) = \left(\frac{a-b\mu_T}{b-c\mu_T}, 0\right)$ fulfills this equation, the tangency equation can be written as

$$\mu_P(\sigma_P) = \frac{a - b\mu_T}{b - c\mu_T} + \frac{\mu_T - \frac{a-b\mu_T}{b-c\mu_T}}{\sigma_T}\sigma_P = \frac{a - b\mu_T}{b - c\mu_T} - \frac{a - 2b\mu_T + c\mu_T^2}{(b - c\mu_T)\sigma_T}\sigma_P\,.$$

This shows that the ordinate of the tangent coincides with the expected return μ_Z of the orthogonal portfolio of T: $\mu_Z = \frac{a-b\mu_T}{b-c\mu_T}$. The construction of tangents to hyperbolas in (μ, σ)-space provides a graphically intuitive interpretation e.g. of determining uncorrelated frontier portfolios.

The following proposition as well as figure 2.3 clarify the economic meaning of the elements of the information matrix.

[2]See e.g. Bronstein, Semendjajew, Musiol, and Mülig (1997, p. 185).

Proposition 2.4 (Information Matrix).
The information matrix $\boldsymbol{A}$ *is fully determined by the expected return and variance of* MVP *and the slope* $\pm\sqrt{d}$ *of the hyperbolas' asymptotes. It provides all necessary information for the relationship of variance and expected return of frontier portfolios. The elements of the information matrix can be interpreted as follows:*

- a *is the square of the maximum mean-volatility ratio of a portfolio:*

$$\max_{\mathbf{x}_P} \frac{\mu_P}{\sigma_P} = \sqrt{a}\ ,$$

  which is attained by a frontier portfolio, say Q. *Portfolio* Q *has expected return* $\mu_Q = a/b$, *variance* $\sigma_Q^2 = a/b^2$, *and composition* $\mathbf{x}_Q = \boldsymbol{V}^{-1}\boldsymbol{\mu}/b$.

- b *is the mean-variance ratio of the* MVP *as well as of portfolio* Q:

$$\frac{\mu_{\mathrm{MVP}}}{\sigma^2_{\mathrm{MVP}}} = \frac{\mu_Q}{\sigma_Q^2} = b\ .$$

- c *is the inverse of the variance of* MVP:

$$\frac{1}{\sigma^2_{\mathrm{MVP}}} = c\ .$$

The information matrix $\boldsymbol{A}$ *is positive definite, specifically*

$$\det(\boldsymbol{A}) = ac - b^2 > 0\ .$$

Proof. Given the expected return and variance of MVP as well as the slope $\sqrt{d}$, the elements of the information matrix are $c = \frac{1}{\sigma^2_{\mathrm{MVP}}}$, $b = \frac{\mu_{\mathrm{MVP}}}{\sigma^2_{\mathrm{MVP}}}$, and $a = d + \frac{b^2}{c}$. The proof of proposition 2.3 shows that $\boldsymbol{A}$ is regular which implies $ac - b^2 > 0$. $\boldsymbol{A}$ is positive definite, since $\det(A) = ac - b^2 > 0$ and $a = \boldsymbol{\mu}'\boldsymbol{V}^{-1}\boldsymbol{\mu} > 0$ holds.

Portfolio Q is defined as the portfolio with maximum mean-volatility ratio. Therefore, it is the tangency portfolio of a tangent in (μ, σ)-space which has an ordinate of zero. In other words, it is orthogonal to a frontier portfolio with zero expected return. Using $\mu_Z = 0$ and equations (2.14) and (2.15) yields the expected return $\mu_Q = a/b$ and variance $\sigma_Q^2 = a/b^2$. The composition $\mathbf{x}_Q$ follows from equation (2.1) and $\mu_Q = a/b$. The other ratios are calculated with equations (2.7) and (2.8). □

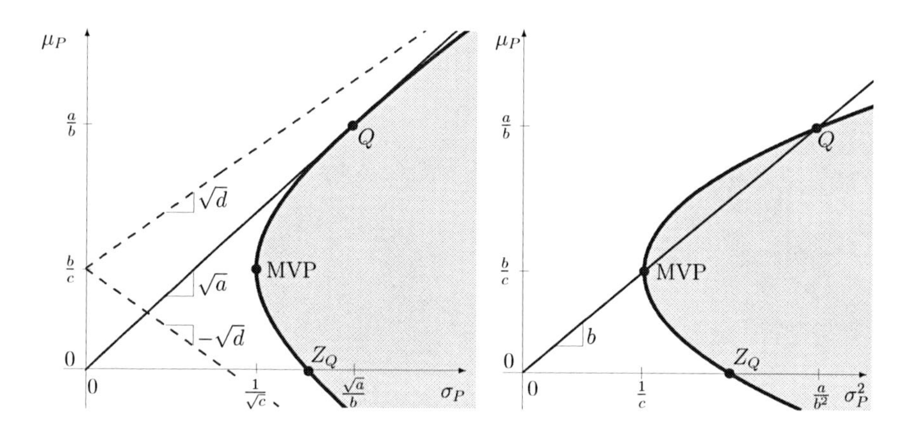

Figure 2.3: Frontier Portfolios and the Elements of the Information Matrix

The shifting strategy

$$\boldsymbol{s} \;=\; \mathbf{x}_{P_2} - \mathbf{x}_{P_1} = \boldsymbol{V}^{-1}(\boldsymbol{\mu}\;\mathbf{1})\boldsymbol{A}^{-1}\begin{pmatrix} \mu_{P_2} - \mu_{P_1} \\ 0 \end{pmatrix} \tag{2.16}$$

reallocates portfolio weights from one frontier portfolio P_1 to another frontier portfolio P_2. It only depends on the difference of expected returns, but does not depend on the original portfolio composition. This implies the *two-fund separation* of frontier portfolios: Given two arbitrary frontier portfolios P_1 and P_2 with $\mu_{P_1} \neq \mu_{P_2}$, any frontier portfolio P_3 can be composed with these two portfolios. The composition is

$$\mathbf{x}_{P_3} = \frac{\mu_{P_3} - \mu_{P_2}}{\mu_{P_1} - \mu_{P_2}} \mathbf{x}_{P_1} + \frac{\mu_{P_1} - \mu_{P_3}}{\mu_{P_1} - \mu_{P_2}} \mathbf{x}_{P_2} ,$$

where the condition $\mu_{P_3} = z\mu_{P_1} + (1-z)\mu_{P_2}$ implies the portion

$$z = \frac{\mu_{P_3} - \mu_{P_2}}{\mu_{P_1} - \mu_{P_2}}$$

that is invested in P_1. Finally, we want to mention that Cochrane (2005) presents a two-fund separation of the frontier with special orthogonal portfolios: Every frontier portfolio can be constructed by a portfolio with minimum second moment and its orthogonal portfolio. Their mean returns are $b/(c + ac - b^2) = \mu_{\text{MVP}}/(1+d)$ and $(1+a)/b$, respectively. Table 2.2 summarizes mean and variance of frontier portfolios with noteworthy properties.[3]

Portfolio risk can be decomposed into risk budgets contributed by each asset. This helps investors to identify the sources of risks and to judge whether a portfolio is diversified or not. Since total portfolio risk can be represented as a sum of the single weighted asset's covariance with the portfolio, $\sigma_P^2 = \mathbf{x}_P' \boldsymbol{V} \mathbf{x}_P = \sum_{i=1}^N x_i (\boldsymbol{V}\mathbf{x}_P)_i = \sum_{i=1}^N x_i \sigma_{i,P}$, the risk budget of the ith asset can be defined as the asset's portion of contribution to total portfolio risk:[4]

$$RB_i \equiv x_i \frac{\sigma_{i,P}}{\sigma_P^2} .$$

[3]The portfolio with maximum mean-variance ratio is derived in proposition 2.13 in the chapter's appendix.

[4]An alternative approach is given by Sharpe (2002, p. 80) who first defines the marginal risk of asset i as $MR_i \equiv \frac{\partial \sigma_P^2}{\partial x_i} = 2\sigma_{i,P}$. Since the weighted marginal risks add to twice the total risk, $\sum_{i=1}^N x_i MR_i = \sum_{i=1}^N x_i \sigma_{i,P} = 2\sigma_P^2$, he defines the risk budget of asset i by $RB_i \equiv \frac{x_i MR_i}{2\sigma_P^2} = \frac{x_i \sigma_{i,P}}{\sigma_P^2}$. Scherer (2004, p. 19) uses the volatility instead of total risk to define the marginal contribution to risk as $MCTR_i \equiv \frac{\partial \sigma_P}{\partial x_i} = \frac{\sigma_{i,P}}{\sigma_P}$. Since the weighted MCTRs add up to the portfolio volatility, $\sum_{i=1}^N x_i MCTR_i = \sum_{i=1}^N x_i \sigma_{i,P}/\sigma_P = \sigma_P$, he refers to the term $x_i \sigma_{i,P}/\sigma_P^2$ as percentage contribution to risk (PCTR).

Table 2.2: Characteristic Portfolios on the Mean-Variance Frontier

Portfolio	expected return and variance of return	portfolio property
Minimum variance portfolio MVP	$\mu_{\text{MVP}} = \frac{b}{c}$ $\sigma^2_{\text{MVP}} = \frac{1}{c}$	mean-variance ratio $\frac{\mu_{\text{MVP}}}{\sigma^2_{\text{MVP}}} = b$
Portfolio with maximum mean-volatility ratio	$\mu_Q = \frac{a}{b}$ $\sigma^2_Q = \frac{a}{b^2}$	mean-volatility ratio $\frac{\mu_Q}{\sigma_Q} = \sqrt{a}$ mean-variance ratio $\frac{\mu_Q}{\sigma^2_Q} = b$
Portfolio with maximum mean-variance ratio	$\mu_P = \frac{\sqrt{a}}{\sqrt{c}}$ $\sigma^2_P = \frac{2a}{ac+b\sqrt{ac}}$	mean-variance ratio $\frac{\mu_P}{\sigma^2_P} = \frac{1}{2}(\sqrt{ac} + b)$
Portfolio with minimum second moment	$\mu_P = \frac{b}{c+ac-b^2}$ $\sigma^2_P = \frac{c+(2+a)(ac-b^2)}{(c+ac-b^2)^2}$	
Orthogonal frontier portfolio of a frontier portfolio Z	$\mu_P = \frac{a-b\mu_Z}{b-c\mu_Z}$ $\sigma^2_P = \frac{a-2b\mu_Z+c\mu^2_Z}{(b-c\mu_Z)^2}$	$\sigma_{P,Z} = 0$

This table provides the expected return and variance of some frontier portfolios with special properties.

The risk budgets add up to one: $\sum_{i=1}^{N} RB_i = 1$. If P is a frontier portfolio, the risk budget of asset i is

$$\begin{aligned} RB_i &= x_i \frac{\sigma_{i,P}}{\sigma^2_P} = \frac{x_i}{\sigma^2_P} \left(\boldsymbol{V}\mathbf{x}_P\right)_i \overset{(2.1)}{=} \frac{x_i}{\sigma^2_P} \left(\begin{pmatrix} \boldsymbol{\mu} & \mathbf{1} \end{pmatrix} \boldsymbol{A}^{-1} \begin{pmatrix} \mu_P \\ 1 \end{pmatrix} \right)_i \\ &= x_i \frac{a - b\mu_i - b\mu_P + c\mu_i\mu_P}{a - 2b\mu_P + c\mu^2_P} , \end{aligned}$$

where $(\cdot)_i$ denotes the ith entry of a vector. The results of mean-variance optimization can be interpreted as implied contributions to expected return and implied risk budgets.[5] As part of the monitoring and revising process of asset management, implied risk budgets can be compared with realized risk proportions after market movements, manager actions, and after updated estimates of return and risk.

[5]See Scherer (2004, p. 20) and Sharpe (2002, p. 80) for reverse optimization and risk analysis based on implied risk budgets.

2.3 Safety First Approach

Critics on volatility as risk measure point out that it measures the spread of the return below as well as above the mean. Many investors rather fear only returns of their portfolio that are below mean or below a target return. This *downside risk* or *(target) shortfall risk* can be measured with the probability $P(R_P < \tau)$ of the portfolio return R_P falling below a target return τ.

Assumption 2.3' (Roy Criterion).
The investor chooses portfolios based on the Roy criterion: Portfolio P_1 is preferred to portfolio P_2 according to the Roy criterion if and only if the probability of falling short a given target return τ is smaller for P_1 than for P_2, i.e. if $P(R_{P_1} < \tau) < P(R_{P_2} < \tau)$.

Roy (1952) introduced the objective of minimizing the shortfall probability as the safety first approach to portfolio selection and derives the optimal portfolio for normally distributed returns. The following assumption is needed for the results in this and the next section.

Assumption 2.4 (Normally Distributed Asset Returns).
The risky asset returns are normally distributed.

Problem 2.5 (Safety First).
Determine the optimal portfolio such that the probability of falling short a target return τ, $\tau < \mu_{\text{MVP}}$, is minimized:

$$\begin{aligned} &\textit{objective:} && \min_{\mathbf{x}_P} P(R_P < \tau) \\ &\textit{constraint:} && \mathbf{x}'_P \mathbf{1} = 1 \quad . \end{aligned}$$

For a normally distributed portfolio return R_P, the probability of falling short a target return τ can be calculated by

$$\begin{aligned} P(R_P < \tau) &= P\left(\frac{R_P - \mu_P}{\sigma_P} < \frac{\tau - \mu_P}{\sigma_P}\right) \\ &= \Phi\left(\frac{\tau - \mu_P}{\sigma_P}\right) = 1 - \Phi\left(\frac{\mu_P - \tau}{\sigma_P}\right), \end{aligned} \tag{2.17}$$

where $\Phi(\cdot)$ denotes the standard normal cumulative distribution function. Since $\Phi(\cdot)$ is increasing, minimizing the target shortfall probability is equivalent to maximizing the ratio $(\mu_P - \tau)/\sigma_P$ of target excess return and standard deviation of portfolio return:

$$\min P(R_P < \tau) \qquad \Longleftrightarrow \qquad \max \frac{\mu_P - \tau}{\sigma_P}. \tag{2.18}$$

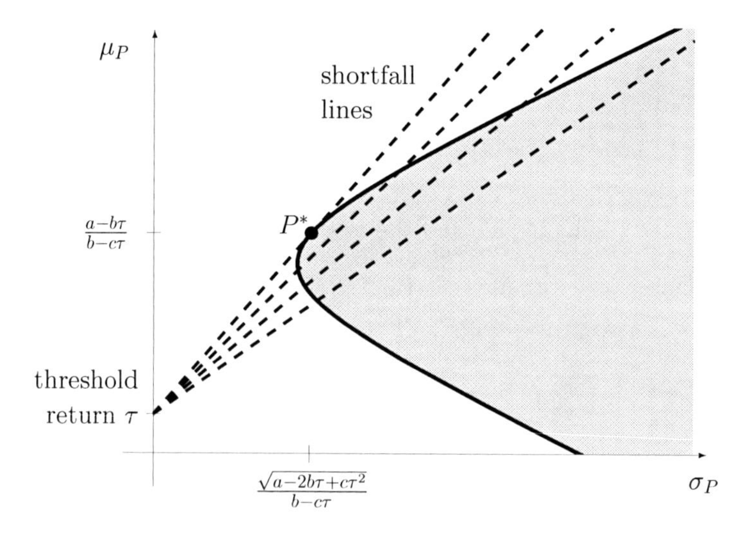

Figure 2.4: Roy's Problem: Minimizing the Threshold Shortfall Probability

Portfolios with equal ratio $(\mu_P - \tau)/\sigma_P$ have an identical target shortfall probability and are located on a straight line in (μ, σ)-space. Figure 2.4 illustrates these so called *(target) shortfall lines.*

Proposition 2.6 (Frontier Portfolio with Minimum Shortfall Probability). *Given a return target τ, $\tau < \mu_{\text{MVP}}$, the efficient frontier portfolio P^* with expected return*

$$\mu_{P^*} = \frac{a - b\tau}{b - c\tau} \tag{2.19}$$

and variance

$$\begin{aligned} \sigma^2_{P^*} &= \frac{a - 2b\tau + c\tau^2}{(b - c\tau)^2} \\ &= \frac{1}{c} + \frac{d}{(b - c\tau)^2} \end{aligned}$$

minimizes the target shortfall probability of the safety first problem 2.5.

Proof. Relation (2.18) shows that minimizing the shortfall probability is equivalent to maximizing the slope of the shortfall line that goes through τ and P in (μ, σ)-space. The tangent on the hyperbola has maximum slope with a tangency portfolio P^* as admissible solution. Therefore, the tangency portfolio P^* on the hyperbola solves problem 2.5. P^* is a frontier portfolio with expected return $\mu_{P^*} = (a - b\tau)/(b - c\tau)$ according to equation (2.14) and its variance can be derived using equation (2.11). □

Equation (2.18) shows that the safety first optimization is related to portfolio optimization with respect to the performance measure Sharpe ratio: If the threshold return τ is chosen equal to the return r_f of the riskless asset, minimizing the shortfall probability is equivalent to maximizing the Sharpe ratio $(\mu_P - r_f)/\sigma_P$ of the portfolio. The portfolio with maximum Sharpe ratio has expected return $(a - br_f)/(b - cr_f)$. This result also holds without the normal distribution assumption 2.4.

2.4 Value at Risk Based Portfolio Selection

Risk measures such as Value at Risk (VaR) have gained much attention recently due to several reasons. With the downturn of equity markets in the year 2001, investors have become more aware of potential downside risks and of the need of portfolio risk measurement. VaR is a standard measure for the determination of the economical capital that banks have to hold to prevent insolvency. The VaR of a portfolio is the estimated maximum loss which cannot be exceeded within a set holding period at a certain confidence level.[6] If ΔV denotes the change in portfolio value within the time period and the confidence level is 99%, then $P(\Delta V < -VaR) = 0.01$ holds. This section shows how to compose a portfolio with minimum VaR and how to maximize the expected return when a VaR limit is given for the case of normally distributed returns.

While the above definition of VaR is used for measuring possible absolute losses, it is more common in portfolio theory to measure losses in relative terms based on portfolio returns. The VaR of a portfolio can be represented by the (disaster or VaR) threshold return τ that the portfolio return possibly falls short. Analogously to the confidence limits, standard shortfall probabilities are $P(R_P < \tau) = 0.01$ or $P(R_P < \tau) = 0.05$. The relation between current portfolio value V, VaR and threshold return is $\tau = -VaR/V$. Kataoka (1963) proposes to maximize the threshold return subject to a given acceptable probability of disaster. Maximizing the threshold return τ for a given shortfall probability p is equivalent to minimizing the VaR at the confidence level $1-p$. In practice of risk controlling divisions, VaR is usually calculated *ex post* based on realized portfolio returns. Since we derive optimal portfolios based on *ex ante* estimates of expected returns and covariances, we continue with the term of threshold

[6]The concept of VaR was introduced by Baumol (1963) as an expected gain-confidence limit criterion for portfolio selection.

return. In the following, we derive the optimal portfolio for an investor who accepts a certain level of shortfall probability and wants to maximize the threshold return.

Assumption 2.3" (Kataoka Criterion).
The investor chooses portfolios based on the Kataoka criterion: Portfolio P_1 is preferred to portfolio P_2 according to the Kataoka criterion if and only if the maximum possible threshold return of P_1 is greater than the one of P_2 for a prespecified shortfall probability.

Problem 2.7 (Minimize VaR).
Determine the optimal portfolio such that the threshold return is maximized for a given shortfall probability:

$$\begin{aligned} \textit{objective:} \quad & \max_{\mathbf{x}_P} \tau \\ \textit{constraint:} \quad & P(R_P < \tau) = p \,. \end{aligned}$$

Rearranging equation (2.17) shows that portfolios with normally distributed returns and identical shortfall probability $p = P(R_P < \tau) = 1 - \Phi\left(\frac{\mu_P - \tau}{\sigma_P}\right)$ are located on a shortfall line with equation $\mu(\sigma_P) = \tau + m_p \sigma_P$ and slope $m_p \equiv \Phi^{-1}(1-p) = (\mu_P - \tau)/\sigma_P$. Alternatively, a portfolio's threshold return for a given shortfall probability p is $\tau = \mu_P - m_p \sigma_P$, where m_p is the $(1-p)$-quantile $\Phi^{-1}(1-p)$ of the standard normal distribution. Figure 2.5 shows increasing thresholds and the corresponding shortfall lines, i.e. portfolios with identical shortfall probability. For a given shortfall probability, the maximum threshold is achieved with a tangency portfolio P on the efficient frontier.[7] A tangency portfolio exists as a solution if the slope of the shortfall line is greater than the slope of the hyperbola's upper asymptote, $m_p > \sqrt{d}$. This is equivalent to the condition that the shortfall probability

[7] Kalin and Zagst (1999, p. 113) refer to portfolio P as the best threshold portfolio. They also investigate distributions for which mean-variance optimization and shortfall risk based portfolio optimization coincide.

satisfies the upper bound $p < \Phi^{-1}\left(-\sqrt{d}\right)$.

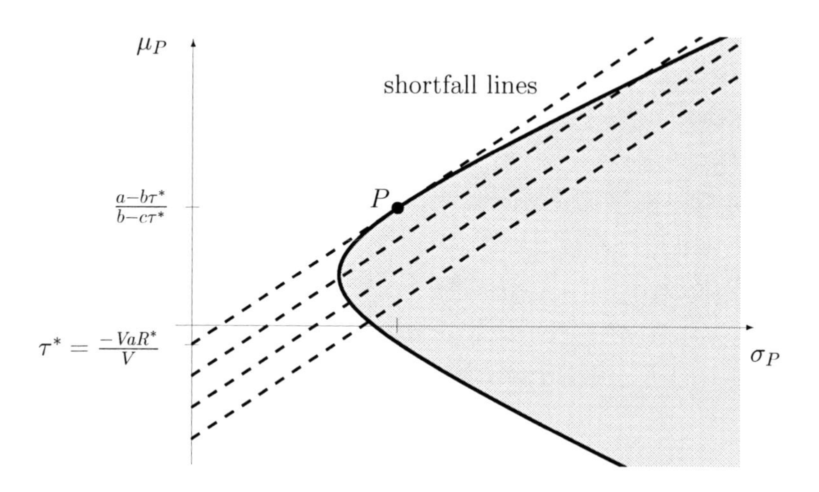

Figure 2.5: Kataoka's Problem: Maximizing the Threshold Return for a Given Shortfall Probability

Proposition 2.8 (Minimum VaR).
Given a shortfall probability p with $p < \Phi\left(-\sqrt{d}\right)$, the maximum threshold return is

$$\tau^* = \mu_{\text{MVP}} - \sqrt{m_p^2 - d}\;\sigma_{\text{MVP}}\,, \tag{2.20}$$

where $m_p \equiv \Phi^{-1}(1-p)$. It is attained with an efficient portfolio with expected return

$$\mu_P = \frac{a - b\tau^*}{b - c\tau^*} = \mu_{\text{MVP}} + \frac{d\sigma_{\text{MVP}}}{\sqrt{m_p^2 - d}}$$

and variance of return

$$\sigma_P^2 = \frac{m_p^2}{m_p^2 - d}\,\sigma_{\text{MVP}}^2\,.$$

Proof. If the threshold return is maximized for a given shortfall probability, the optimal portfolio is an efficient frontier portfolio. Rearranging the shortfall line equation $\mu_P = \tau + m_p\, \sigma_P$ for the threshold and using equation (2.2), the threshold return τ can be represented as a function of the expected return of the frontier portfolio

$$\tau = \mu_P - m_p \sigma_P = \mu_P - m_p \frac{\sqrt{a - 2b\mu_P + c\mu_P^2}}{\sqrt{ac - b^2}} \,.$$

The first order condition $\partial\tau/\partial\mu_P = 0$ yields the expected return of the frontier portfolio that corresponds to the maximum threshold. Its variance of return can be calculated with equation (2.2). □

Finally, let's consider the case that both threshold return and shortfall probability are fixed. A typical example is a company that wants to keep its rating constant. The rating reflects its probability for an insolvency and default might be triggered by a return below a disaster threshold return. If a certain rating or a default probability is accepted, an investor's objective might be maximizing the expected return.

Assumption 2.3''' (Telser Criterion).
The investor chooses portfolios based on the Telser criterion: Portfolio P_1 is preferred to portfolio P_2 according to the Telser criterion if and only if both portfolios have at most a prespecified shortfall probability for a given threshold return and the expected return of P_1 is greater than the expected return of P_2.

Problem 2.9 (Maximize Expected Return Given Shortfall Probability).
Determine the optimal portfolio such that the expected return is maximized for a given threshold and threshold shortfall probability:

$$\begin{aligned} \textit{objective:} \quad & \max_{\mathbf{x}_P} \mu_P \\ \textit{constraint:} \quad & P(R_P < \tau) \leq p \,. \end{aligned} \tag{2.21}$$

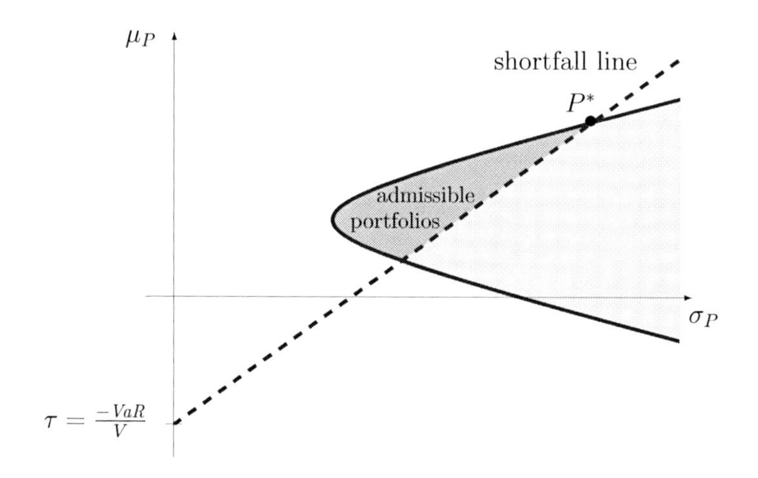

Figure 2.6: Telser's Problem: Maximizing the Expected Return Given the Threshold Shortfall Probability

Figure 2.6 illustrates the set of admissible portfolios as well as the optimal portfolio with maximum expected return.

Proposition 2.10.
A solution of problem 2.9 exists if $p \geq \Phi\left(-\sqrt{a - 2b\tau + c\tau^2}\right)$. *The optimal portfolio of problem 2.9 is an efficient frontier portfolio with expected return and volatility*

$$\mu_{P^*} = \frac{bm_p^2 - (ac - b^2)\tau + m_p\left((ac - b^2)(a - 2b\tau + c\tau^2 - m_p^2)\right)^{\frac{1}{2}}}{cm_p^2 - ac + b^2}$$

$$\sigma_{P^*} = \frac{(b - c\tau)m_p + \left((ac - b^2)(a - 2b\tau + c\tau^2 - m_p^2)\right)^{\frac{1}{2}}}{cm_p^2 - ac + b^2}.$$

Proof. Let T_τ denote the tangency portfolio with respect to τ. T_τ has the least shortfall probability according to proposition 2.6. The admissible set of portfolios for condition $P(R_P < \tau)$ is nonempty if T_τ is admissible, i.e. if

$$\begin{aligned} p \geq P(R_{T_\tau} < \tau) &= P\left(\frac{R_{T_\tau} - E[R_{T_\tau}]}{\sigma_{T_\tau}} < \frac{\tau - E[R_{T_\tau}]}{\sigma_{T_\tau}}\right) \\ &= \Phi\left(-\sqrt{a - 2b\tau + c\tau^2}\right) , \end{aligned}$$

where μ_{T_τ} and $\sigma^2_{T_\tau}$ are given by equations (2.14) and (2.15).

The optimal portfolio P^* of problem 2.9 is located at the intersection of the efficient frontier and the shortfall line. The expected portfolio returns and volatilities of the points of intersection are

$$\begin{aligned} \mu_P &= \frac{bm_p^2 - (ac - b^2)\tau \pm m_p\left((ac - b^2)(a - 2b\tau + c\tau^2 - m_p^2)\right)^{\frac{1}{2}}}{cm_p^2 - ac + b^2} \\ \sigma_P &= \frac{(b - c\tau)m_p \pm \left((ac - b^2)(a - 2b\tau + c\tau^2 - m_p^2)\right)^{\frac{1}{2}}}{cm_p^2 - ac + b^2} . \end{aligned}$$

They are derived from the condition $m_p \equiv \Phi^{-1}(1 - p) = (\mu_P - \tau)/\sigma_P$ given by equation (2.17) after using equations (2.11) and (2.12). Given $P^* \neq T_\tau$, there are two points of intersection and the frontier portfolio with the highest expected return is the optimal solution. □

2.5 The Efficient Frontier Given a Riskless Asset

This section derives the relationship of return and total risk of efficient portfolios when a riskless investment is available and the investor chooses portfolios according to the mean-variance criterion in assumption 2.3. In order to include a riskless asset to the asset universe, assumption 2.2 is to be replaced by

Assumption 2.2' (Riskless and Risky Assets).
There are n risky assets and one riskless asset with rate r_f that are traded in the market. The risky asset returns R_i, $i = 1, \ldots, n$, have expected return $\boldsymbol{\mu} = (\mu_1, \ldots, \mu_n)'$ and positive definite covariance matrix $\boldsymbol{V}$. There are at least two risky assets with differing expected returns.

The combination of a portfolio of risky assets with a riskless asset yields a linear relationship of expected return and portfolio volatility. Let x_{r_f} denote the proportion of wealth that is invested in the riskless investment. Then, the expected return and volatility of a portfolio P consisting of the riskless asset and a portfolio S of risky assets read

$$\mu_P = x_{r_f} r_f + (1 - x_{r_f})\mu_S = \mu_S + x_{r_f}(r_f - \mu_S) \quad (2.22)$$

$$\sigma_P = \left(x_{r_f}^2 \cdot 0 + (1 - x_{r_f})^2 \sigma_S^2\right)^{\frac{1}{2}} = |1 - x_{r_f}|\sigma_S \,. \quad (2.23)$$

Solving equation (2.23) for $x_{r_f} = 1 \mp \frac{\sigma_P}{\sigma_S}$ and inserting in equation (2.22) yields the expected return

$$\mu_P = \left(1 \mp \frac{\sigma_P}{\sigma_S}\right) r_f \pm \frac{\sigma_P}{\sigma_S}\mu_S = r_f \pm \frac{\mu_S - r_f}{\sigma_S}\sigma_P$$

which is maximized if the Sharpe ratio $\frac{\mu_S - r_f}{\sigma_S}$ of portfolio S is maximized.[8]

[8] Sharpe (1966, p. 123) introduced this performance measure as reward-to-variability ratio.

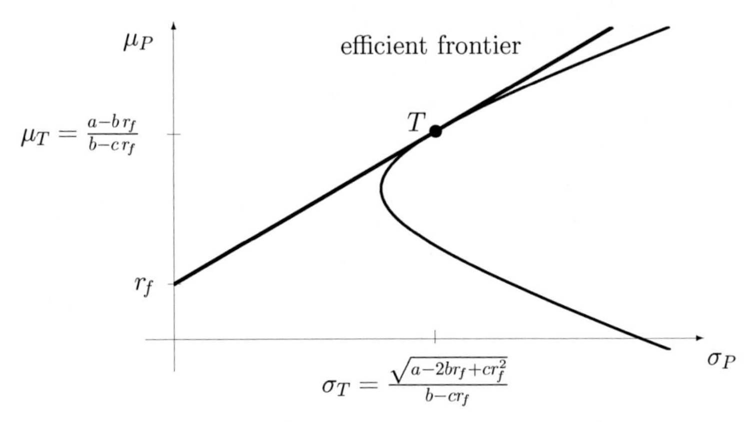

Figure 2.7: Frontier Portfolios Given a Riskless Asset

The maximum is attained if the riskless asset is combined with the corresponding tangency portfolio T:

$$\begin{aligned} \mu_P &= r_f + \frac{\mu_T - r_f}{\sigma_T}\sigma_P \\ &= r_f + \sqrt{a - 2br_f + cr_f^2}\,\sigma_P\,, \end{aligned} \tag{2.24}$$

where the expected portfolio return $\mu_T = \frac{a-br_f}{b-cr_f}$ and variance of return $\sigma_T^2 = \frac{a-2br_f+cr_f^2}{(b-cr_f)^2}$ are given by equations (2.14) and (2.15). The Sharpe ratio of an efficient portfolio is $\frac{\mu_P - r_f}{\sigma_P} = \frac{\mu_T - r_f}{\sigma_T} = \sqrt{a - 2br_f + cr_f^2}$. The efficient frontier is illustrated in figure 2.7.

As a result, a *two-fund separation* of the efficient frontier also holds in the presence of a riskless investment: Every efficient portfolio can be constructed with the riskless asset and the tangency portfolio. The two-step procedure of composing an individual efficient portfolio is known as *Tobin-separation*: Tobin (1958) proposes to determine foremost the tangency portfolio that corresponds to the riskless investment. Second, the tangency portfolio and riskless investment are combined in order to fit the individual investor's risk-return preference.

2.6 Example: Global Asset Allocation

This section illustrates the models presented above with an example of global asset allocation. We consider the case of a global asset manager investing capital to the following six major asset classes: Canadian, French, German, Japanese, U.K., and U.S. equity market. We assume that he is able to invest directly in national indices and estimates expected returns and covariances based on historic returns. The historic data set consists of monthly returns of MSCI indices during the time period January 1970 to December 2006.

National equity indices data and riskfree rates were compiled on January 12, 2007 from two sources: Data on national indices is retrieved from MSCI. Total return indices (Gross Index) are used in order to include price performance as well as income from dividend payments. The income from dividends is reinvested in the index and contributes to the total index performance. The chosen reinvestment methodology is "gross daily total return" which approximates the maximum possible dividend reinvestment without including tax credits nor withholding tax on dividends. All indices are USD denominated. In 37 years, 444 monthly returns of each index are observed during the time period January 1970 to December 2006. Figure 2.8 illustrates the gross indices of the six countries. Returns of the 3-month US treasury bill are used as riskless rates. The annualized means, standard deviations, covariances, and correlations are given in table 2.3.

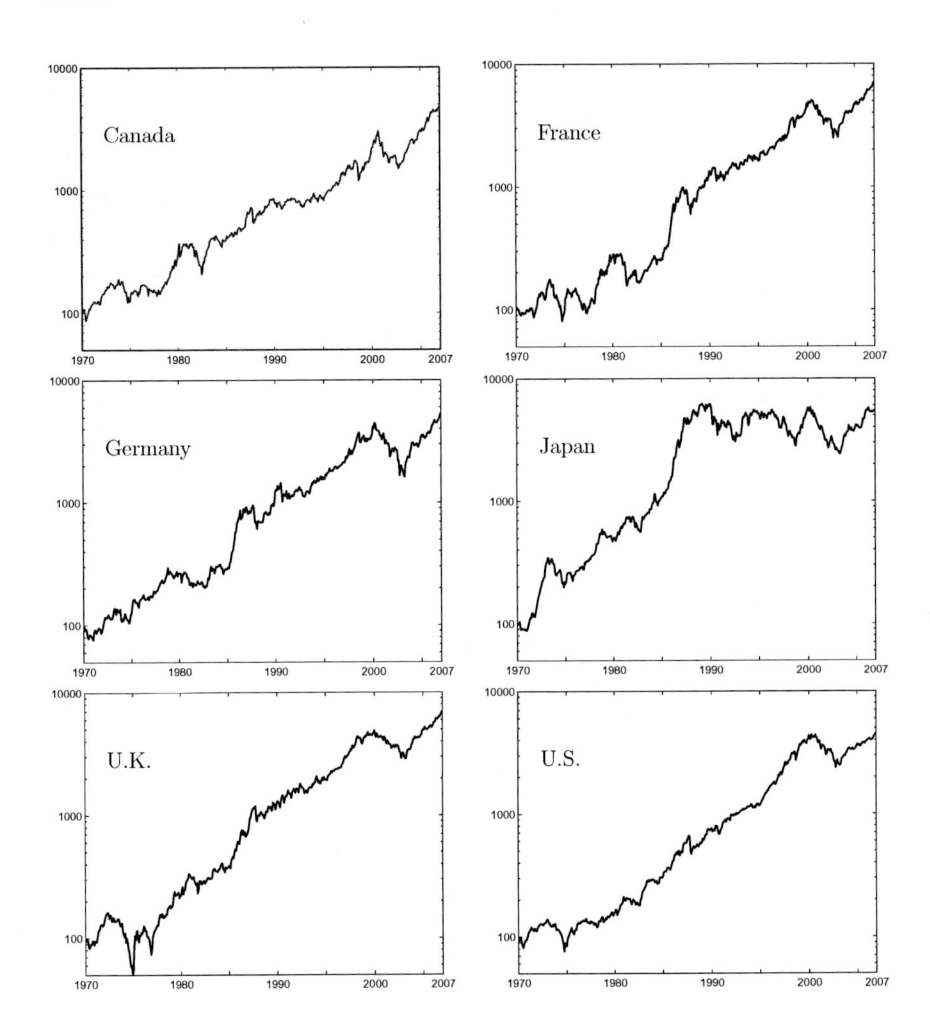

Figure 2.8: MSCI Gross Indices USD Denominated, Log Scale

Source: MSCI. The MSCI data contained herein is the property of Morgan Stanley Capital International Inc. (MSCI). MSCI, its affiliates and information providers make no warranties with respect to any such data. The MSCI data contained herein is used under license and may not be further used, distributed or disseminated without the express written consent of MSCI.

Table 2.3: Annualized Mean, Standard Deviation, Covariance, and Correlation of Monthly Returns of 6 Indices, January 1970 – December 2006

	mean return	standard deviation	covariance Canada	France	Germany	Japan	U.K.	U.S.
Canada	0.1227	0.1904	0.03590	0.02024	0.01610	0.01379	0.02185	0.02067
France	0.1404	0.2228	0.02024	0.04933	0.03102	0.01934	0.02834	0.01668
Germany	0.1305	0.2118	0.01610	0.03102	0.04458	0.01670	0.02198	0.01481
Japan	0.1331	0.2219	0.01379	0.01934	0.01670	0.04894	0.01818	0.01022
U.K.	0.1393	0.2248	0.02185	0.02834	0.02198	0.01818	0.05028	0.01799
U.S.	0.1149	0.1524	0.02067	0.01668	0.01481	0.01022	0.01799	0.02305

	mean return	standard deviation	correlation Canada	France	Germany	Japan	U.K.	U.S.
Canada	0.1227	0.1904	1.0000	0.4809	0.4025	0.3291	0.5143	0.7185
France	0.1404	0.2228	0.4809	1.0000	0.6614	0.3936	0.5691	0.4947
Germany	0.1305	0.2118	0.4025	0.6614	1.0000	0.3576	0.4642	0.4619
Japan	0.1331	0.2219	0.3291	0.3936	0.3576	1.0000	0.3665	0.3043
U.K.	0.1393	0.2248	0.5143	0.5691	0.4642	0.3665	1.0000	0.5283
U.S.	0.1149	0.1524	0.7185	0.4947	0.4619	0.3043	0.5283	1.0000

Figure 2.9 plots the 6 country indices, some portfolios of two indices as well as the frontier in (μ, σ)-space. The figure on the right illustrates the asymptotes of the hyperbola as well as the frontier portfolios MVP and Q. Given the annualized mean $\boldsymbol{\mu}$ and covariance matrix $\boldsymbol{V}$ from table 2.3, the information matrix for frontier portfolios is

$$\boldsymbol{A} = \begin{pmatrix} 0.7885 & 6.3113 \\ 6.3113 & 52.0737 \end{pmatrix}$$

and $d = a - b^2/c = 0.0236$.

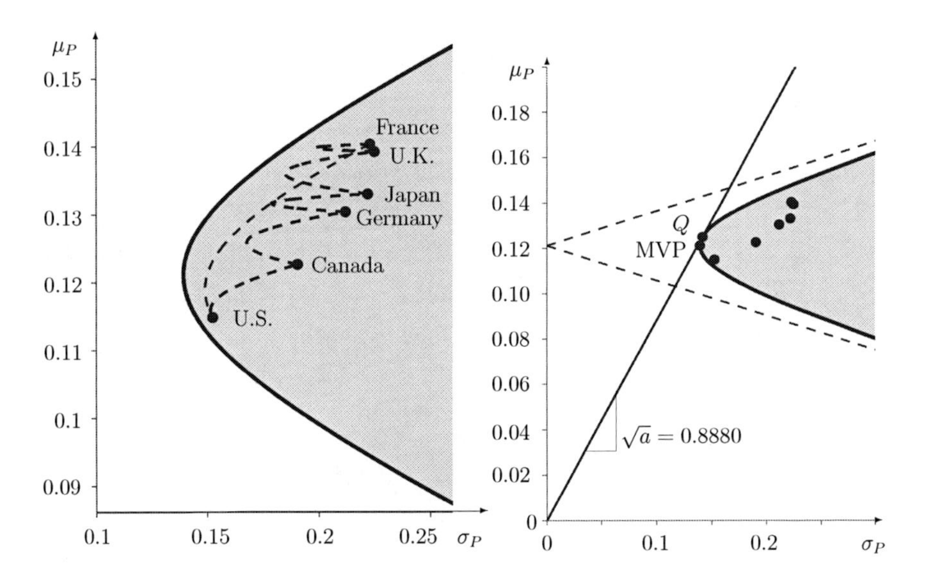

Figure 2.9: Six Country Indices in (μ, σ)-Space: (a) Frontier Portfolios and Portfolios of Two Indices; (b) The Maximum Return-Volatility Ratio

The minimum variance portfolio has expected return $\mu_{\text{MVP}} = b/c = 0.1212$ and volatility $\sigma_{\text{MVP}} = 1/\sqrt{c} = 0.1386$. Portfolio Q has maximum mean-volatility ratio $\sqrt{a} = 0.8880$. The mean-variance ratio of portfolios MVP and Q is $\mu_{\text{MVP}}/\sigma^2_{\text{MVP}} = \mu_Q/\sigma^2_{\text{MVP}} = b = 6.3113$. The slope of the asymptotes of the hyperbola is $\sqrt{d} = 0.1535$.

An efficient frontier portfolio with expected return μ_P has composition

$$\mathbf{x}_P = \boldsymbol{V}^{-1}(\boldsymbol{\mu}\ \ \mathbf{1})\boldsymbol{A}^{-1}\begin{pmatrix}\mu_P\\1\end{pmatrix} = \begin{pmatrix} 5.0056 & -0.5723\\ 18.4966 & -2.2500\\ -1.5960 & 0.3265\\ 4.8904 & -0.3880\\ 17.4278 & -2.0937\\ -44.2244 & 5.9775 \end{pmatrix}\begin{pmatrix}\mu_P\\1\end{pmatrix},$$

see equation (2.1). Table 2.4 provides the compositions of the portfolios MVP and Q. It also shows the optimal portfolio selection for the problems 2.5, 2.7, and 2.9 when, respectively, a threshold return $\tau = -0.20$, the shortfall probability $P(R_P < \tau) = 0.05$, or when both threshold return $\tau = -0.20$ and shortfall probability $P(R_P < -0.20) = 0.05$ are given. Reallocating assets from one frontier portfolio to another frontier portfolio and increasing the expected return about 1% is achieved with the self-financing shifting strategy $\boldsymbol{s} = (0.0501\ \ 0.1850\ \ -0.0160\ \ 0.0489\ \ 0.1743\ \ -0.4422)'$.

Table 2.4: Optimal Portfolio Selection with 6 Country Indices

	MVP	Q	P_1	P_2	P_3
mean return μ_P	0.1212	0.1249	0.1226	0.1232	0.1454
standard deviation σ_P	0.1386	0.1407	0.1389	0.1392	0.2100
composition $\mathbf{x}_P$:					
Canada	0.0344	0.0531	0.0414	0.0444	0.1556
France	−0.0082	0.0608	0.0178	0.0286	0.4397
Germany	0.1331	0.1272	0.1309	0.1299	0.0945
Japan	0.2047	0.2229	0.2116	0.2144	0.3231
U.K.	0.0185	0.0836	0.0431	0.0533	0.4405
U.S.	0.6175	0.4525	0.5552	0.5294	−0.4534
$P(R_P < -0.2000)$	0.01023	0.01046	0.01009	0.01012	0.05000
$P(R_P <$ -0.1057 $)$	0.05074	0.05055	0.05006	0.05000	0.11585

This table shows the mean return, standard deviation, composition, and the shortfall probability of mean-variance efficient frontier portfolios. The portfolios are the minimum variance portfolio MVP, portfolio Q with maximum mean-volatility ratio, and the solutions P_1, P_2, P_3 of problems 2.5, 2.7, and 2.9. The solution P_1 of Roy's safety first problem 2.5 is calculated for the threshold return $\tau = -0.20$. It has minimum shortfall probability $P(R_{P_1} < -0.20) = 0.01009$. For a given shortfall probability $P(R_{P_2} < \tau^*) = 0.05$, portfolio P_2 solves Kataoka's problem 2.7 with maximum threshold $\tau^* = -0.1057$. For a threshold return $\tau = -0.20$ and a given shortfall probability $P(R_{P_3} < -0.20) = 0.05$, the optimal portfolio P_3 of the Telser problem 2.9 has maximum expected return $\mu_{P_3} = 0.1454$.

Appendix

This appendix recalls the Karush-Kuhn-Tucker conditions. We also derive the expected return and variance of the portfolio with maximum mean-variance ratio.

We first consider an optimization problem of the following form:

Problem 2.11 (Convex Problem).
Let f and $\boldsymbol{g} = (g_1, \ldots, g_n)'$ be differentiable convex functions and let $\boldsymbol{h} = (h_1, \ldots, h_m)'$ be an affine function. Then, find the optimal $\mathbf{x}^*$ such that f is minimized under constraints:

$$\begin{aligned} \textit{objective:} \quad & \min_{\mathbf{x}} f(\mathbf{x}) \\ \textit{constraints:} \quad & \boldsymbol{g}(\mathbf{x}) \leq \mathbf{0} \\ & \boldsymbol{h}(\mathbf{x}) = \mathbf{0}\ . \end{aligned}$$

The Karush-Kuhn-Tucker conditions are necessary conditions for the optimality of a solution of the convex problem. They appeared first in Karush's (1939) unpublished master's thesis and were published in Kuhn and Tucker (1950). The following condition ensures that a solution is non-degenerate in the sense that it does not only depend on the constraints but also on the properties of the function f: There exists a point $\mathbf{x}$ such that $g_i(\mathbf{x}) < 0$ for all $i = 1, \ldots, n$ (Slater's constraint qualification).

Proposition 2.12 (Karush-Kuhn-Tucker).
Let Slater's constraint qualification be satisfied. The convex problem 2.11 has solution $\mathbf{x}^*$ if and only if there exist constants $\boldsymbol{u} = (u_1, \ldots, u_n)'$, $\boldsymbol{v} = (v_1, \ldots, v_m)'$ such that the Karush-Kuhn-Tucker (KKT) conditions

hold:

$$
\begin{array}{rcll}
\frac{\partial f}{\partial \mathbf{x}}(\mathbf{x}^*) + \sum_{i=1}^n u_i \frac{\partial g_i}{\partial \mathbf{x}}(\mathbf{x}^*) + \sum_{j=1}^m v_j \frac{\partial h_j}{\partial \mathbf{x}}(\mathbf{x}^*) & = & \mathbf{0} & \text{(optimality condition)} \\
\boldsymbol{g}(\mathbf{x}^*) & \leq & \mathbf{0} & \text{(feasibility condition)} \\
\boldsymbol{h}(\mathbf{x}^*) & = & \mathbf{0} & \text{(feasibility condition)} \\
i = 1, \ldots, n: \ u_i g_i(\mathbf{x}^*) & = & 0 & \text{(complementary} \\
 & & & \text{slackness condition)} \\
\boldsymbol{u} & \geq & \mathbf{0} & \text{(non-negativity cond.)} \ .
\end{array}
$$

Proof. See e.g. Jarre and Stoer (2004, pp. 229–233). □

The Karush-Kuhn-Tucker conditions generalize the *method of Lagrange multipliers*: Given the absence of inequality constraints $\boldsymbol{g}(\mathbf{x}) \leq \mathbf{0}$, the problem 2.11 has solution $\mathbf{x}^*$ if and only if there exist constants $\boldsymbol{v} = (v_1, \ldots, v_m)'$ such that $\frac{\partial L}{\partial \mathbf{x}}(\mathbf{x}^*, \boldsymbol{v}) = \mathbf{0}$ and $\boldsymbol{h}(\mathbf{x}^*) = \mathbf{0}$ hold where the Lagrange function is defined by $L(\mathbf{x}, \boldsymbol{v}) \equiv f(\mathbf{x}) + \sum_{j=1}^m v_j h(\mathbf{x})$.

The following proposition derives the portfolio with maximum mean-variance ratio that is mentioned in table 2.2.

Proposition 2.13.

The maximum of the ratio of expected return and variance, μ_P/σ_P^2, is $(\sqrt{ac} + b)/2$. It is achieved with an efficient frontier portfolio P with expected return $\mu_P = \sqrt{a/c}$ and variance of return $\sigma_P^2 = \frac{2\sqrt{a}}{c\sqrt{a}+b\sqrt{c}}$.

Proof. The first order condition for the extremum

$$
\frac{\partial \frac{\mu_P}{\sigma_P^2}}{\partial \mu_P} = \frac{(ac - b^2)(a - c\mu_P^2)}{(a - 2b\mu_P + c\mu_P^2)^2} = 0
$$

has solutions $\mu_P = \pm\frac{\sqrt{a}}{\sqrt{c}}$, $\sigma_P^2 \overset{(2.2)}{=} \frac{2a \mp 2b\sqrt{\frac{a}{c}}}{ac - b^2} = \frac{2\sqrt{a}}{c\sqrt{a} \pm b\sqrt{c}}$. The maximum is obtained with $\mu_P = \sqrt{a/c}$ and $\sigma_P^2 = 2\sqrt{a}/(c\sqrt{a} + b\sqrt{c})$, because the second derivative

$$
\frac{\partial^2 \frac{\mu_P}{\sigma_P^2}}{\partial \mu_P^2}\left(\frac{\sqrt{a}}{\sqrt{c}}\right) = \frac{2(ac - b^2)(2ab - 3ac\mu_P + c^2\mu_P^3)}{(a - 2b\mu_P + c\mu_P^2)^3} = \frac{a(ac - b^2)(b - \sqrt{ac})}{2(a - b\sqrt{\frac{a}{c}})^3}
$$

is negative due to $ac > b^2$. The frontier portfolio is efficient, since $ac > b^2$ is equivalent to $\sqrt{a}/\sqrt{c} > b/c$ which shows that $\mu_P > \mu_{\text{MVP}}$. $\square$

Chapter 3

Benchmark-Relative Portfolio Selection

A standard approach to assess a portfolio manager's success in portfolio management is to measure the portfolio performance relative to a benchmark portfolio. Given portfolio and benchmark returns R_P and R_B, the difference of their returns $R_P - R_B$ is a standard measure of relative performance. The expected value of this return difference is called *active return*, *benchmark excess return*, or *gain*, and its volatility is called *active risk* or *tracking error*. Tracking error volatility indicates how close the portfolio tracks a benchmark. Portfolio managers compete in improving portfolio returns. Performance based salaries provide an incentive to managers to increase the active return by increasing active risk. Therefore, active risk is usually restricted by constraints on tracking error and partly on portfolio beta and total risk in practice of active fund management.

This chapter derives closed form solutions when portfolios are composed relative to a benchmark portfolio. Section 3.1 recalls the benchmark-relative portfolio selection when the tracking error is minimized given an expected excess return as well as when the excess return is maximized under a tracking error constraint. The portfolio selection with an additional constraint on portfolio beta is discussed in section 3.2. Section 3.3 shows how to optimally constrain the tracking error and beta simultaneously such that the portfolio manager composes mean-variance efficient portfolios.

3.1 Constraint on Tracking Error

Active portfolio management is typically restricted in the extend of deviations from a strategic benchmark. This section studies the portfolios selection of managers who maximize benchmark excess return given a tracking error constraint. We show that this problem is related to Roll's (1992) problem of minimizing the tracking error for a given expected benchmark excess return.

Whenever a portfolio manager deviates from the composition of the benchmark portfolio, two aspects are of interest: Active risk and active return, or in other words, tracking error and excess return. Given the shifting strategy $\boldsymbol{s} \equiv \mathbf{x}_P - \mathbf{x}_B$ that shifts the benchmark allocation $\mathbf{x}_B$ to an active portfolio allocation $\mathbf{x}_P = \mathbf{x}_B + \boldsymbol{s}$, the expected benchmark excess return is $G \equiv \mu_P - \mu_B = \boldsymbol{\mu}'\mathbf{x}_P - \boldsymbol{\mu}'\mathbf{x}_B = \boldsymbol{\mu}'\boldsymbol{s}$ and the tracking error is $\sigma_s^2 \equiv \boldsymbol{s}'\boldsymbol{V}\boldsymbol{s}$. The shifting strategy is denoted with $\boldsymbol{s}$ instead of $\mathbf{x}$ to stress that it is self financing: $\boldsymbol{s}'\mathbf{1} = \sum_{i=1}^{n} s_i = 0$. Roll (1992) calls $\boldsymbol{s}$ the alteration vector. In the following, we derive optimal solutions for the shifting strategy.

Given the standard assumptions 2.1 (frictionless market) and 2.2 (risky asset returns), we derive the optimal portfolio selection of a portfolio manager with one of the following objectives:

Assumption 3.1 (TEV Criterion).
The agent minimizes the tracking error for a given expected benchmark excess return.

Assumption 3.1' (Maximize Excess Return).
The agent maximizes the expected benchmark excess return under given risk constraints.

The corresponding portfolio selection problems are called TEV problem due to the relevance of the tracking error volatility.

Problem 3.1 (TEV Problem).
Given a benchmark portfolio B with $\mu_B > \mu_{\mathrm{MVP}}$ and an expected excess return G with $G \geq 0$, determine the shifting strategy such that the tracking error is minimized. Alternatively, if the tracking error is given, determine a shifting strategy such that the expected excess return is maximized:

$$\begin{array}{llrcl} (1) & \textit{objective:} & \min\limits_{s} \sigma_s^2 & & \\ & \textit{constraints:} & \boldsymbol{s}'\boldsymbol{\mu} & = & G \\ & & \boldsymbol{s}'\boldsymbol{1} & = & 0 \end{array} \qquad \begin{array}{llrcl} (2) & \textit{objective:} & \max\limits_{s} \boldsymbol{s}'\boldsymbol{\mu} & & \\ & \textit{constraints:} & \boldsymbol{s}'\boldsymbol{V}\boldsymbol{s} & = & \sigma_s^2 \\ & & \boldsymbol{s}'\boldsymbol{1} & = & 0 \end{array} .$$

Roll (1992) shows that minimizing tracking error as is specified in TEV problem 3.1(1) does not produce better managed portfolios, since the active portfolio is as inefficient as the benchmark. So, minimizing tracking error should not be a primary aim in portfolio selection. However, since tracking error restrictions are often used as tactical or active risk budgets and performance of portfolio managers is often measured based on benchmark excess returns, the second type of TEV problem 3.1(2) is important in practice of active portfolio management. Jorion (2003) shows that TEV-constrained portfolios are located on an ellipse in (μ, σ^2)-space. Figure 3.1 illustrates TEV portfolios with identical tracking error in (μ, σ)-space and plots the location of portfolios with maximum benchmark excess return given a tracking error constraint. The following proposition presents the solution of the TEV problem. It shows that Roll's (1992) and Jorion's (2003) solution of the TEV problems 3.1(1) and 3.1(2) coincide if the benchmark excess return and the tracking error constraint of the two

TEV problems are chosen specifically.

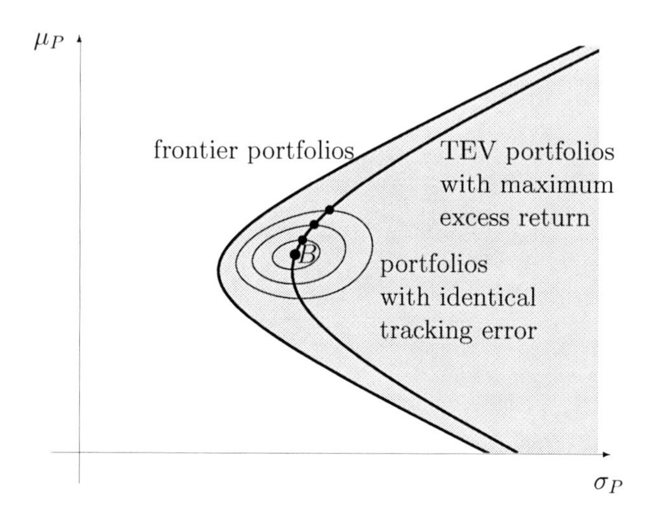

Figure 3.1: Iso-Tracking Error Curves and TEV Portfolios

Proposition 3.2 (TEV Portfolio).
For $G = \sqrt{d}\ \sigma_s$, the solutions of both TEV problems 3.1(1) and 3.1(2) coincide. The solution of the TEV problem is called TEV portfolio and is given by $\mathbf{x}_P = \mathbf{x}_B + \boldsymbol{s}$ with optimal shifting strategy

$$\boldsymbol{s} \;=\; \boldsymbol{V}^{-1}(\boldsymbol{\mu}\ \mathbf{1})\boldsymbol{A}^{-1}\begin{pmatrix} G \\ 0 \end{pmatrix} = \frac{1}{\sqrt{d}}\boldsymbol{V}^{-1}\left(\boldsymbol{\mu} - \mu_{\mathrm{MVP}}\mathbf{1}\right)\sigma_s\ . \qquad (3.1)$$

The shifting strategy $\boldsymbol{s}$ is independent of the benchmark. The excess return $\boldsymbol{s}'\boldsymbol{\mu}$ is linear in tracking error volatility

$$\boldsymbol{s}'\boldsymbol{\mu} = \sqrt{d}\,\sigma_s\ , \qquad (3.2)$$

which implies that the information ratio of the optimal shifting strategy is independent of the tracking error: $IR \equiv \boldsymbol{s}'\boldsymbol{\mu}/\sigma_s = \sqrt{d}$. The TEV portfolio has expected return $\mu_P = \mu_B + \sqrt{d}\,\sigma_s$ and variance

$$\sigma_P^2 \;=\; \sigma_B^2 + \frac{2}{\sqrt{d}}(\mu_B - \mu_{\mathrm{MVP}})\sigma_s + \sigma_s^2\ . \qquad (3.3)$$

Proof. Roll (1992, equations A-1, A-2) provides the solution of the optimal shifting strategy $\boldsymbol{s} = \boldsymbol{V}^{-1}(\boldsymbol{\mu}\ \ \mathbf{1})\boldsymbol{A}^{-1}(G\ \ 0)'$. It can be derived analogously to the frontier portfolio composition $\mathbf{x}_P$ in the proof of proposition 2.3 with $\mathbf{x}_P$ and the sum of portfolio weights, 1, replaced by $\boldsymbol{s}$ and 0, respectively. Furthermore, we have

$$\begin{aligned}\boldsymbol{A}^{-1}\begin{pmatrix} G \\ 0 \end{pmatrix} &= \frac{1}{\det \boldsymbol{A}}\begin{pmatrix} c & -b \\ -b & a \end{pmatrix}\begin{pmatrix} G \\ 0 \end{pmatrix} = \frac{1}{ac-b^2}\begin{pmatrix} cG \\ -bG \end{pmatrix} \\ &= \frac{1}{d}\begin{pmatrix} G \\ -\frac{b}{c}G \end{pmatrix}.\end{aligned}$$

For $G = \max \boldsymbol{\mu}'\boldsymbol{s} = \sqrt{d}\sigma_s$, Roll's and Jorion's (2003, equation B3) solution coincide:

$$\begin{aligned}\boldsymbol{s} &= \boldsymbol{V}^{-1}(\boldsymbol{\mu}\ \ \mathbf{1})\boldsymbol{A}^{-1}\begin{pmatrix} G \\ 0 \end{pmatrix} = \frac{1}{d}\boldsymbol{V}^{-1}(\boldsymbol{\mu}\ \ \mathbf{1})\begin{pmatrix} G \\ -\frac{b}{c}G \end{pmatrix} \\ &= \frac{1}{\sqrt{d}}\boldsymbol{V}^{-1}\left(\boldsymbol{\mu} - \frac{b}{c}\mathbf{1}\right)\sigma_s\,. \qquad (3.4)\end{aligned}$$

The self-financing shifting strategy $\boldsymbol{s}$ is independent of the benchmark, since none of the benchmark's characteristics appears in the formula above. The optimal strategy's information ratio $IR = \boldsymbol{s}'\boldsymbol{\mu}/\sigma_s = \sqrt{d}$ is independent of the tracking error. The variance of the TEV portfolio is

$$\begin{aligned}\sigma_P^2 &= (\mathbf{x}_B + \boldsymbol{s})'\boldsymbol{V}(\mathbf{x}_B + \boldsymbol{s}) = \mathbf{x}_B'\boldsymbol{V}\mathbf{x}_B + 2\mathbf{x}_B'\boldsymbol{V}\boldsymbol{s} + \boldsymbol{s}'\boldsymbol{V}\boldsymbol{s} \\ &= \sigma_B^2 + \frac{2}{\sqrt{d}}(\mu_B - \mu_{\mathrm{MVP}})\,\sigma_s + \sigma_s^2\,,\end{aligned}$$

where equation (3.4), $\mathbf{x}_B'\boldsymbol{\mu} = \mu_B$, $\mathbf{x}_B'\mathbf{1} = 1$, and $b/c = \mu_{\mathrm{MVP}}$ are used to derive the covariance term

$$2\mathbf{x}_B'\boldsymbol{V}\boldsymbol{s} = \frac{2}{\sqrt{d}}\mathbf{x}_B\boldsymbol{V}\boldsymbol{V}^{-1}(\boldsymbol{\mu} - \mu_{\mathrm{MVP}}\mathbf{1})\sigma_s = \frac{2}{\sqrt{d}}(\mu_B - \mu_{\mathrm{MVP}})\,\sigma_s\,.$$

□

The strategy (3.1) for shifting among TEV portfolios is identical to the shifting strategy (2.16) for reallocations among frontier portfolios. Then, the TEV portfolio is efficient if and only if the benchmark portfolio is efficient. Furthermore, the TEV portfolio is as inefficient as the benchmark portfolio in terms of difference of variance: $\sigma_P^2 - \sigma_{P*}^2 \overset{(3.3)}{=} \sigma_B^2 - \sigma_{B*}^2$, where the star indicates a frontier portfolio with identical expected return. This shows that the TEV line is the mean-variance frontier shifted to the right in (μ, σ^2)-space. Equation (3.3) can be rearranged to provide the TEV line

$$\mu_P = \mu_{\text{MVP}} + \sqrt{(\mu_B - \mu_{\text{MVP}})^2 + d(\sigma_P^2 - \sigma_B^2)}\,,$$

where $\sigma_s = G/\sqrt{d} = (\mu_P - \mu_B)/\sqrt{d}$ is used. The slope of the tangency of the TEV line in TEV portfolio P is given by

$$\frac{\partial \mu_P}{\partial \sigma_P} = \frac{d\sigma_P}{\sqrt{(\mu_B - \mu_{\text{MVP}})^2 + d(\sigma_P^2 - \sigma_B^2)}}\,. \tag{3.5}$$

If portfolio managers are only restricted by a tracking error constraint, they will simply maximize expected return for a given tracking error and compose TEV portfolios. As a result, the manager chooses active risk equal to the tracking error constraint. Since the active portfolio has greater total risk than the benchmark, it does not dominate the benchmark by the mean-variance criterion. In other words, some frontier portfolios dominate the active portfolio based on total portfolio risk. However, if risk is measured as volatility of excess returns, the TEV portfolios have minimum tracking error and are therefore efficient in excess-mean-variance space but not in mean-variance space.

3.2 Constraints on Tracking Error and Beta

Imposing an additional constraint on portfolio beta can reduce the active portfolio's inefficiency, as is is shown by Roll (1992). This section presents an alternative proof of Roll's optimal benchmark-relative portfolio selection when tracking error is minimized under an additional restriction on portfolio beta. We show that the solutions of this TEVBR problem for varying excess return coincide with the solutions of maximizing excess return when beta is fixed and tracking error volatility is varied.

Portfolios that allow the holding of cash can be characterized by portfolio beta to specify the amount of market risk exposure. A low portfolio beta and high amount of wealth hold in cash is preferable specifically in down turning markets. In the following, funds are considered that consist of risky assets only and for which cash holdings are prohibited. Adding a constraint on beta aims at reducing total portfolio risk by restricting systematic risk.

Problem 3.3 (TEVBR Problem).
Given a benchmark portfolio B with $\mu_B > \mu_{\mathrm{MVP}}$, a portfolio beta $\beta_{P,B}$ and an expected excess return G with $G \geq 0$, determine the shifting strategy such that the tracking error is minimized. Alternatively, if the tracking error and portfolio beta is given, determine a shifting strategy such that the expected excess return is maximized:

$$
\begin{array}{llcl@{\qquad}llcl}
(1) & \textit{objective:} & \min\limits_{\boldsymbol{s}} \sigma_s^2 & & (2) & \textit{objective:} & \max\limits_{\boldsymbol{s}} \boldsymbol{s}'\boldsymbol{\mu} & \\
 & \textit{constraints:} & \frac{\mathbf{x}_P'\boldsymbol{V}\mathbf{x}_B}{\mathbf{x}_B'\boldsymbol{V}\mathbf{x}_B} = & \beta_{P,B} & & \textit{constraints:} & \frac{\mathbf{x}_P'\boldsymbol{V}\mathbf{x}_B}{\mathbf{x}_B'\boldsymbol{V}\mathbf{x}_B} = & \beta_{P,B} \\
 & & \boldsymbol{s}'\boldsymbol{\mu} = & G & & & \boldsymbol{s}'\boldsymbol{V}\boldsymbol{s} = & \sigma_s^2 \\
 & & \boldsymbol{s}'\mathbf{1} = & 0 & & & \boldsymbol{s}'\mathbf{1} = & 0\,.
\end{array}
$$

Figure 3.2 illustrates TEVBR portfolios for standard beta constraints. The solution of this problem can be stated in a form similar to the composition of a frontier portfolio in equation (2.1) by extending the information

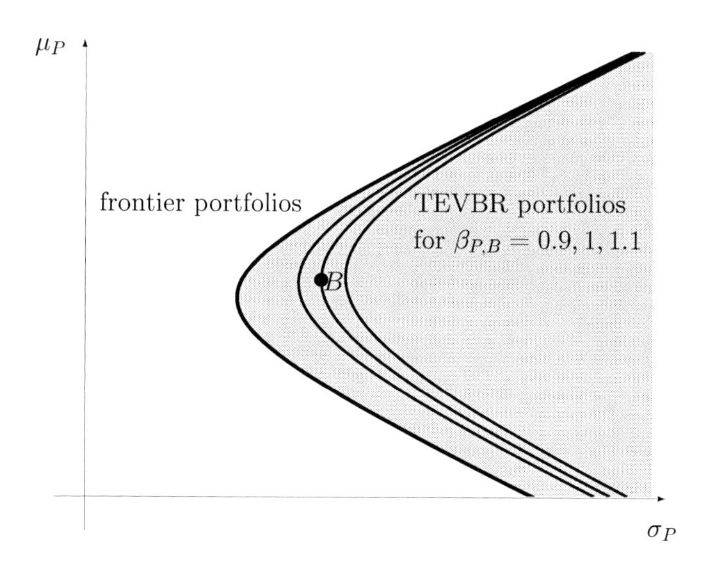

Figure 3.2: TEVBR Portfolios for Standard Beta Constraints and Varying Tracking Error Constraints

matrix to a matrix containing benchmark characteristics. The *generalized information matrix* $\boldsymbol{H}$ is defined by

$$\begin{aligned} \boldsymbol{H} &\equiv \begin{pmatrix} \mathbf{x}_B'\boldsymbol{V} \\ \boldsymbol{\mu}' \\ \mathbf{1}' \end{pmatrix} \boldsymbol{V}^{-1}(\boldsymbol{V}\mathbf{x}_B \;\; \boldsymbol{\mu} \;\; \mathbf{1}) \\ &= \begin{pmatrix} \sigma_B^2 & \mu_B & 1 \\ \mu_B & a & b \\ 1 & b & c \end{pmatrix}. \end{aligned} \tag{3.6}$$

Its inverse $\boldsymbol{H}^{-1}$ is given by

$$\boldsymbol{H}^{-1} = \frac{1}{\det \boldsymbol{H}} \begin{pmatrix} ac - b^2 & b - c\mu_B & -a + b\mu_B \\ b - c\mu_B & -1 + c\sigma_B^2 & \mu_B - b\sigma_B^2 \\ -a + b\mu_B & \mu_B - b\sigma_B^2 & -\mu_B^2 + a\sigma_B^2 \end{pmatrix},$$

where the determinant of $\boldsymbol{H}$ is

$$\det \boldsymbol{H} = -a + 2b\mu_B - c\mu_B^2 + (ac - b^2)\sigma_B^2 \,. \tag{3.7}$$

The determinant of the generalized information matrix can be interpreted as a measure of the inefficiency of the benchmark. As can be seen from $\det \boldsymbol{H} \overset{(2.2)}{=} (ac - b^2)(\sigma_B^2 - \sigma_{B^*}^2)$, the determinant provides a measure for the difference of variance between the benchmark and the efficient frontier portfolio B^* that has identical expected return $\mu_{B^*} = \mu_B$. Roll (1980) introduces the matrix $\boldsymbol{H}$ for the representation of orthogonal portfolios, but it is not used when Roll (1992) derives the solution of problem 3.3(1). We provide an alternative proposition and proof in matrix notation that is based on the generalized information matrix. This approach reveals some similarities of the equations (2.16), (3.1), and (3.8) below for the composition of shifting strategies among frontier, TEV, and TEVBR portfolios.

Proposition 3.4 (TEVBR Portfolio).
The solution of problem 3.3(1) or 3.3(2) is called TEVBR portfolio and is given by $\mathbf{x}_P = \mathbf{x}_B + \boldsymbol{s}$ *with optimal shifting strategy*

$$\boldsymbol{s} = \boldsymbol{V}^{-1}\left(\boldsymbol{V}\mathbf{x}_B \;\; \boldsymbol{\mu} \;\; \mathbf{1}\right)\boldsymbol{H}^{-1}\begin{pmatrix}(\beta_{P,B}-1)\sigma_B^2\\ G\\ 0\end{pmatrix}. \tag{3.8}$$

The minimum tracking error variance is

$$\begin{aligned}\sigma_s^2 &= \begin{pmatrix}(\beta_{P,B}-1)\sigma_B^2\\ G\\ 0\end{pmatrix}' \boldsymbol{H}^{-1}\begin{pmatrix}(\beta_{P,B}-1)\sigma_B^2\\ G\\ 0\end{pmatrix}\\ &= \frac{(\sigma_B^2 - \sigma_{\mathrm{MVP}}^2)G^2 - 2G(\mu_B - \mu_{\mathrm{MVP}})(\beta_{P,B}-1)\sigma_B^2 + d(\beta_{P,B}-1)^2\sigma_B^4}{\sigma_{\mathrm{MVP}}^2 \det \boldsymbol{H}}\,.\end{aligned} \tag{3.9}$$

The variance of return of the active portfolio is

$$\sigma_P^2 \;=\; (2\beta_{P,B}-1)\sigma_B^2+\sigma_s^2\,. \tag{3.10}$$

TEVBR problem 3.3(2) with constraints on portfolio beta and tracking error has optimal shifting strategy $\boldsymbol{s}$ *given by equation (3.8), where the maximum excess return* $\max_{\boldsymbol{s}} \boldsymbol{s}'\boldsymbol{\mu}$ *is given by*

$$G=\frac{(\mu_B-\mu_{\mathrm{MVP}})(\beta_{P,B}-1)\sigma_B^2+\sqrt{\sigma_{\mathrm{MVP}}^2\det\boldsymbol{H}((\sigma_B^2-\sigma_{\mathrm{MVP}}^2)\sigma_s^2-(1-\beta_{P,B})^2\sigma_B^4)}}{\sigma_B^2-\sigma_{\mathrm{MVP}}^2}. \tag{3.11}$$

Proof. First, we rewrite the first constraint

$$\beta_{P,B}=\frac{\mathbf{x}_P'\boldsymbol{V}\mathbf{x}_B}{\mathbf{x}_B'\boldsymbol{V}\mathbf{x}_B}=\frac{(\mathbf{x}_B+\boldsymbol{s})'\boldsymbol{V}\mathbf{x}_B}{\mathbf{x}_B'\boldsymbol{V}\mathbf{x}_B}=1+\frac{\boldsymbol{s}'\boldsymbol{V}\mathbf{x}_B}{\mathbf{x}_B'\boldsymbol{V}\mathbf{x}_B}$$

of problem 3.3(1) as $\boldsymbol{s}'\boldsymbol{V}\mathbf{x}_B=\sigma_B^2(\beta_{P,B}-1)$. Then, the Lagrange function of the TEVBR problem 3.3(1) is

$$L(\mathbf{x},\boldsymbol{\lambda})=\boldsymbol{s}'\boldsymbol{V}\boldsymbol{s}+\lambda_1(\sigma_B^2(\beta_{P,B}-1)-\boldsymbol{s}'\boldsymbol{V}\mathbf{x}_B)+\lambda_2(G-\boldsymbol{s}'\boldsymbol{\mu})-\lambda_3\boldsymbol{s}'\mathbf{1}\,.$$

The first order condition $\frac{\partial L}{\partial \boldsymbol{s}}=2\boldsymbol{V}\boldsymbol{s}-\lambda_1\boldsymbol{V}\mathbf{x}_B-\lambda_2\boldsymbol{\mu}-\lambda_3\mathbf{1}=0$ yields

$$\boldsymbol{s} \;=\; \frac{1}{2}\boldsymbol{V}^{-1}(\lambda_1\boldsymbol{V}\mathbf{x}_B+\lambda_2\boldsymbol{\mu}+\lambda_3\mathbf{1})=\frac{1}{2}\boldsymbol{V}^{-1}(\boldsymbol{V}\mathbf{x}_B\;\;\boldsymbol{\mu}\;\;\mathbf{1})\begin{pmatrix}\lambda_1\\ \lambda_2\\ \lambda_3\end{pmatrix}. \tag{3.12}$$

Multiplying both sides from the left with $(\boldsymbol{V}\mathbf{x}_B\;\;\boldsymbol{\mu}\;\;\mathbf{1})'$ yields

$$\begin{pmatrix}\mathbf{x}_B'\boldsymbol{V}\\ \boldsymbol{\mu}'\\ \mathbf{1}'\end{pmatrix}\boldsymbol{s} \;=\; \frac{1}{2}\begin{pmatrix}\mathbf{x}_B'\boldsymbol{V}\\ \boldsymbol{\mu}'\\ \mathbf{1}'\end{pmatrix}\boldsymbol{V}^{-1}(\boldsymbol{V}\mathbf{x}_B\,\boldsymbol{\mu}\,\mathbf{1})\begin{pmatrix}\lambda_1\\ \lambda_2\\ \lambda_3\end{pmatrix}=\frac{1}{2}\boldsymbol{H}\begin{pmatrix}\lambda_1\\ \lambda_2\\ \lambda_3\end{pmatrix}$$

and this equation together with the constraints can be solved for the Lagrange multipliers

$$\begin{pmatrix}\lambda_1\\ \lambda_2\\ \lambda_3\end{pmatrix} \;=\; 2\boldsymbol{H}^{-1}\begin{pmatrix}\mathbf{x}_B'\boldsymbol{V}\\ \boldsymbol{\mu}'\\ \mathbf{1}'\end{pmatrix}\boldsymbol{s}=2\boldsymbol{H}^{-1}\begin{pmatrix}\sigma_B^2(\beta_{P,B}-1)\\ G\\ 0\end{pmatrix}.$$

Finally, using the Lagrange multipliers in equation (3.12), the solution (3.8) is given.

The tracking error variance shrinks from a long equation down to

$$\begin{aligned}
\sigma_s^2 &= \boldsymbol{s}'\boldsymbol{V}\boldsymbol{s} \\
&\overset{(3.8)}{=} \begin{pmatrix} (\beta_{P,B}-1)\sigma_B^2 \\ G \\ 0 \end{pmatrix}' \boldsymbol{H}^{-1}(\boldsymbol{V}\mathbf{x}_B\ \boldsymbol{\mu}\ \mathbf{1})'\boldsymbol{V}^{-1}\boldsymbol{V} \\
&\quad \cdot \boldsymbol{V}^{-1}(\boldsymbol{V}\mathbf{x}_B\ \ \boldsymbol{\mu}\ \ \mathbf{1})\,\boldsymbol{H}^{-1}\begin{pmatrix} (\beta_{P,B}-1)\sigma_B^2 \\ G \\ 0 \end{pmatrix} \\
&\overset{(3.6)}{=} \begin{pmatrix} (\beta_{P,B}-1)\sigma_B^2 \\ G \\ 0 \end{pmatrix}' \boldsymbol{H}^{-1} \begin{pmatrix} (\beta_{P,B}-1)\sigma_B^2 \\ G \\ 0 \end{pmatrix} \\
&= \frac{c(\sigma_B^2-\frac{1}{c})G^2 - 2cG(\frac{b}{c}-\mu_B)(1-\beta_{P,B})\sigma_B^2 + c(a-\frac{b^2}{c})(\beta_{P,B}-1)^2\sigma_B^4}{\det \boldsymbol{H}} \\
&= \frac{(\sigma_B^2-\sigma_{\text{MVP}}^2)G^2 - 2G(\mu_B-\mu_{\text{MVP}})(\beta_{P,B}-1)\sigma_B^2 + d(\beta_{P,B}-1)^2\sigma_B^4}{\sigma_{\text{MVP}}^2 \det \boldsymbol{H}} .
\end{aligned}$$

Using the first constraint on the covariance $\mathbf{x}_B'\boldsymbol{V}\boldsymbol{s} = (\beta_{P,B}-1)\sigma_B^2$, the variance of return of the active portfolio can be simplified to

$$\begin{aligned}
\sigma_P^2 &= \mathbf{x}_P'\boldsymbol{V}\mathbf{x}_P = (\mathbf{x}_B+\boldsymbol{s})'\boldsymbol{V}(\mathbf{x}_B+\boldsymbol{s}) = \sigma_B^2 + 2\mathbf{x}_B'\boldsymbol{V}\boldsymbol{s} + \sigma_s^2 \\
&= (2\beta_{P,B}-1)\sigma_B^2 + \sigma_s^2 .
\end{aligned}$$

Given the second type of TEVBR problem with constraints on portfolio beta and tracking error variance, equation (3.9) can be solved for the corresponding excess return

$$G = \frac{(\mu_B-\mu_{\text{MVP}})(\beta_{P,B}-1)\sigma_B^2 + \sqrt{\sigma_{\text{MVP}}^2 \det \boldsymbol{H}((\sigma_B^2-\sigma_{\text{MVP}}^2)\sigma_s^2 - (1-\beta_{P,B})^2\sigma_B^4)}}{\sigma_B^2-\sigma_{\text{MVP}}^2} .$$

□

3.3 Using Constraints to Reduce Inefficiency

One might claim that adding constraints to a portfolio optimization problem is expected to restrict the set of possible solutions and therefore to deteriorate the optimal solution. However, additional constraints can also be used to reduce the inefficiency of the portfolio. Jorion (2003) shows that imposing an additional constraint on total risk may improve the performance of the tracking error restricted portfolio selection. This section derives the optimal combination of constraints on portfolio beta and tracking error such that the benchmark-relative portfolio selection yields a mean-variance efficient portfolio.

The following proposition derives the optimal active and beta risk budgets for achieving efficient portfolios with benchmark-relative portfolio selection.

Proposition 3.5 (Efficient TEVBR Portfolio).
Given a benchmark portfolio B with $\mu_B > \mu_{\text{MVP}}$ and a benchmark excess return G, the TEVBR problem 3.3(2) yields a mean-variance efficient portfolio P^* with $\mu_{P^*} = \mu_B + G$ if the constraints are set to

$$\begin{aligned}
\beta_{P^*,B} &= \frac{a - 2b\mu_B + c\mu_B^2 + (c\mu_B - b)G}{(ac - b^2)\sigma_B^2} = \frac{\sigma_{B^*}^2}{\sigma_B^2} + \frac{(\mu_B - \mu_{\text{MVP}})}{d\sigma_B^2} G \\
\sigma_s^2 &= \sigma_B^2 - \frac{a - 2b\mu_B + c\mu_B^2 - cG^2}{ac - b^2} = \sigma_B^2 - \sigma_{B^*}^2 + \frac{G^2}{d} \,,
\end{aligned}$$

where B^* denotes the frontier portfolio with expected return $\mu_{B^*} = \mu_B$.

Proof. First, we present the optimal portfolio P^* and derive its beta and tracking error. Second, using this risk budgets as constraints, we show that P^* solves the TEVBR problem. The composition $\mathbf{x}_{P^*}$ of the efficient frontier portfolio P^* with expected return $\mu_{P^*} = \mu_B + G$ is given by equation (2.1). Using equations (2.1), (2.13), and (2.2), the portfolio beta is

$$\begin{aligned}
\beta_{P^*,B} &= \frac{\mathbf{x}'_{P^*}\boldsymbol{V}\mathbf{x}_B}{\mathbf{x}'_B\boldsymbol{V}\mathbf{x}_B} = \frac{(\mu_{P^*} \;\; 1)\boldsymbol{A}^{-1}\begin{pmatrix}\boldsymbol{\mu}' \\ \mathbf{1}'\end{pmatrix}\boldsymbol{V}^{-1}\boldsymbol{V}\mathbf{x}_B}{\sigma_B^2} \\
&= \frac{(\mu_B + G \;\; 1)\boldsymbol{A}^{-1}\begin{pmatrix}\boldsymbol{\mu}' \\ \mathbf{1}'\end{pmatrix}\mathbf{x}_B}{\sigma_B^2} = \frac{(\mu_B + G \;\; 1)\boldsymbol{A}^{-1}\begin{pmatrix}\mu_B \\ 1\end{pmatrix}}{\sigma_B^2} \\
&= \frac{\frac{a-b(\mu_B+G)-b\mu_B+c(\mu_B+G)\mu_B}{ac-b^2}}{\sigma_B^2} = \frac{a - 2b\mu_B + c\mu_B^2 + G(c\mu_B - b)}{(ac-b^2)\sigma_B^2} \\
&= \frac{\sigma_{B^*}^2}{\sigma_B^2} + \frac{G(\mu_B - \mu_{\mathrm{MVP}})}{d\sigma_B^2}\,.
\end{aligned}$$

The tracking error variance of P^* is the variance of the shifting strategy $\boldsymbol{s} = \mathbf{x}_{P^*} - \mathbf{x}_B$:

$$\begin{aligned}
\sigma_s^2 &= \boldsymbol{s}'\boldsymbol{V}\boldsymbol{s} = (\mathbf{x}_{P^*} - \mathbf{x}_B)'\boldsymbol{V}(\mathbf{x}_{P^*} - \mathbf{x}_B) \\
&= \mathbf{x}'_{P^*}\boldsymbol{V}\mathbf{x}_{P^*} - 2\mathbf{x}'_{P^*}\boldsymbol{V}\mathbf{x}_B + \mathbf{x}'_B\boldsymbol{V}\mathbf{x}_B \\
&= \frac{a - 2b(\mu_B + G) + c(\mu_B + G)^2}{ac - b^2} \\
&\quad -2\frac{a - b(\mu_B + G) - b\mu_B + c(\mu_B + G)\mu_B}{ac - b^2} + \sigma_B^2 \\
&= \sigma_B^2 - \frac{a - 2b\mu_B + c\mu_B^2 - cG^2}{ac - b^2} = \sigma_B^2 - \sigma_{B^*}^2 + \frac{G^2}{d}\,.
\end{aligned}$$

If these two risk constraints are used in problem 3.3(2), equation (3.10) yields the total risk of the TEVBR portfolio

$$\begin{aligned}
\sigma_P^2 &= (2\beta_{P,B} - 1)\sigma_B^2 + \sigma_s^2 \\
&= \left(2\frac{a - 2b\mu_B + c\mu_B^2 + G(c\mu_B - b)}{ac - b^2} - 1\right)\sigma_B^2 + \sigma_B^2 \\
&\quad - \frac{a - 2b\mu_B + c\mu_B^2 - cG^2}{ac - b^2} \\
&= \frac{a - 2b(\mu_B + G) + c(\mu_B + G)^2}{ac - b^2}\,,
\end{aligned}$$

which is identical to the variance of the frontier portfolio with expected return $\mu_B + G$. $\square$

Chapter 4

Delegated Investing and Safety First Approach

A standard assumption in portfolio theory is that there is only one investor who decides on everything concerning financial investments. Delegation of asset management can not be studied based on this standard assumption, since at least one who delegates and one who manages the portfolio is needed. Delegated investing is the principal's transfer of responsibility of decision making on financial investments to an agent. This chapter presents a model with a principal who delegates portfolio selection to a financial professional and makes use of risk budgeting. The principal pursues a safety first approach and controls the agent's portfolio selection with benchmark tracking constraints. An optimal constraint on tracking error ensures that the agent produces a second-best solution. Given sufficient information and the possibility to additionally restrict portfolio beta, the delegated portfolio selection yields a first-best solution.

This chapter also could have been titled "Delegated Investing and Maximizing Sharpe Ratio". This is a direct consequence of the fact shown in section 2.3 that the safety first approach yields a portfolio with maximum Sharpe ratio if returns are normally distributed and the riskless return is chosen as threshold return, i.e. $\tau = r_f$. The derived optimal portfolios outperform a benchmark in terms of Sharpe ratio. The interpretation in terms of Sharpe ratio maximization is left to the reader. The chapter provides the interpretations for the safety first approach solely.

4.1 Principal-Agent Problems of Delegating Investment Decisions

Financial institutions such as banks, pension funds, and insurance funds play a more or less important role in several ways in most people's life. Many private investors delegate investment decisions on the majority of their wealth to institutional investors. Despite that financial institutions really do matter, they seem to be less important in financial theory. It is a common standard assumption that investors invest their wealth directly at financial markets. The delegation process is often ignored. Financial institutions come into play when market frictions are considered. They have advantages in costs that are connected with investing in financial markets. They have less transaction costs or costs on gathering financial information due to scale effects. It is the assumption of frictionless markets and homogeneous information that permits scientific papers to ignore them. There is a discrepancy that delegated investing does matter but is neglected in financial theory. Allen (2001) stresses the need for more research on delegated investing: "There is an inconsistency in assuming that when you give your money to a financial institution there is no agency problem, but when you give it to a firm there is."

The focus of corporate finance is the agency problem of an investor giving money to a firm and how she can ensure that managers act on her behalf. For the purpose of a simple linguistic differentiation, the principal and the agent are assumed to be a female and a male person, respectively. More generally, principal-agent models are concerned with problems that arise when a principal hires an agent under conditions of asymmetric information. One strand of principal-agent theory studies the implications of the information asymmetry stemming from the principal's difficulty of monitoring the agent's actions or characteristics.[1] The unobservability of the agent's hidden action is the origin of the "moral hazard" problem that the agent maximizes rather his own utility than the principal's one. The agent is not interested in choosing the first-best solution which is the solution that maximizes the principal's utility. Instead, he maximizes the compensation payment of his employment contract. The principal is restricted to solutions that are achievable through contracts and that the agent provides. Among these restricted alternatives, the one that maximizes the principals utility is called second-best solution. To find the optimal contract for a second-best solution is the main challenge of principal-agent problems. Problems that are concerned with the optimal contract design can further be distinguished in models with managers that have or do not have private information. In models with private information, managers receive private signals or have superior forecast ability.[2] When agents do not have private information, information asymmetry may be introduced with an uninformed investor who lacks information that is common to financial professionals. Besides the search for the optimal contract, one of the central questions in these models is: Which information is sufficient to be able to achieve a second-best or even a first-best solution?

A special principal-agent relationship arises when the optimal portfolio selection is delegated. The principal could be a private investor who wants her wealth to be managed professionally or as well the senior management of a fund who hires a portfolio manager. This principal-agent relationship

[1]Classical principal-agent problems that are concerned with manager effort, output, and compensation are analyzed e.g. by Ross (1973), Jensen and Meckling (1976), and Mirrlees (1976, 1999).

[2]See e.g. Admati and Pfleiderer (1997) and Stoughton (1993).

is typically subject to the following challenges: First, the agent's effort or success to act on the principal's behalf needs to be measured in order to implement a performance-stimulating remuneration. Even if the agent reveals his action, i.e. the composition of a portfolio of assets, the principal might not have enough information to be able to judge his contribution. Second, the agent usually does not want to disclose the composition of the selected portfolio and – to a lesser extend – share the information which the selection is based upon. Even if the portfolio composition is disclosed, additional information is necessary to judge the agent's performance. Instead, compensation is often based on benchmark excess returns which are easy to measure. Then third, a benchmark portfolio needs to be specified that suits the principal's objective. Fourth, upscaling of benchmark excesss return by simply leveraging the benchmark and excessive risk-taking should be prevented with portfolio constraints. She also might use the portfolio constraints to control the portfolio selection for the benefit of her objectives.[3]

Reasons for delegating are e.g. the superior knowledge and lower transaction costs that financial institutions have, capacity limits for financial decision making, or simply shifting the responsibility of financial success to someone else. In the following, we focus on problems originating from differing objectives between principal and agent in portfolio selection. The investor's objectives are often well represented in terms of absolute objectives. Poor portfolio performance is specifically evident if the return of the delegated investment falls below certain thresholds such as minimum return guarantees or returns of investments like government bonds. There are also psychological important thresholds such as zero return or the inflation rate which stand for nominal and real maintenance of invested capital. Threshold returns are usually set to a negative value in stop-loss-strategies.

[3]In Kraft and Korn (2007), a sufficient statistic for the principal to obtain the first-best solution is the final value of the "growth optimal portfolio" in a continuous-time model.

Underperforming a benchmark can often be accepted a few times, but returns falling below these thresholds often trigger regret and considerations to rethink the delegation. Therefore, this chapter investigates the safety first approach of minimizing the threshold shortfall probability when investment decisions are delegated. Stracca (2005) reviews principal-agent models of delegated portfolio management and concludes: "Another interesting extension appears to be considering less standard utility functions for principals, say shortfall risk, which may be again particularly relevant in the pension fund industry."

4.2 Strategic and Tactical Asset Allocation

This section discusses the possible organizational setup of the management of a fund and the role of strategic and tactical asset allocation. A three-tier governance structure is outlined that is concerned with the strategical and tactical asset allocation as well as with risk allocation in the investment process.

Fund management aims to meet specified investment objectives of private or institutional clients. A sound organizational design and corporate governance is necessary to be able to efficiently satisfy the commitments. The delegation of investment authority for managing a fund can be organized around three basic types of investment decisions:[4]

- long-term strategic decisions e.g. made by an oversight committee or a board of trustees,
- medium-term tactical decisions by an investment committee,
- short-term trading decisions delegated to portfolio managers.

[4]Cardon and Coche (2004) present a three-tier governance structure for central banks. Ho (2004) illustrates a three-level framework of risk management for the exchange fund of Hong Kong's foreign reserves portfolio.

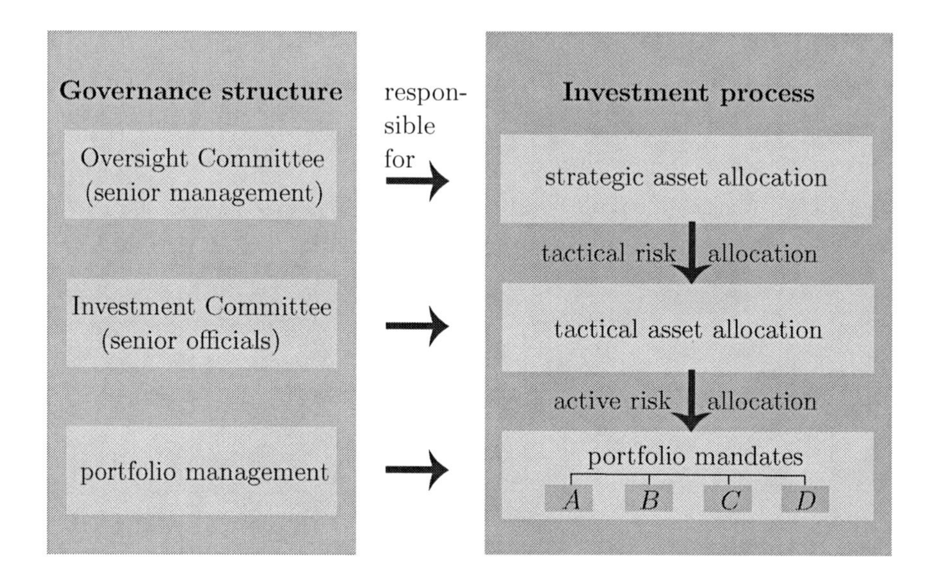

Figure 4.1: Three-Tier Organizational Set-up of Investment Management
Source: Following Cardon and Coche (2004, p. 15).

The governance structure of a managed fund should represent the organizational framework of an efficient investment decision process. Figure 4.1 illustrates a typical three-tier organizational set-up of delegating investment decisions. First, the oversight committee or the board of trustees of the fund decides about the strategic policy or strategic allocation of a fund's assets across major asset classes. Then, a layer of tactical asset allocation and a layer of actual portfolio mandates is added in order to benefit from medium-term and short-term investment opportunities. Alternatively, a two-tier organizational set-up without the second or third layer is also suitable to combine passive and active portfolio management. The common target of these governance structures is to improve the risk-return profile of the strategic asset allocation with shorter termed investments.

The board of trustees of a fund is responsible for overseeing generally the management, activities, and affairs of a fund. Members of the board of trustees may usually group a oversight committee that is responsible for the long-term implementation of the fund's strategic policy. The main instrument for implementing the investor's long-term objective is the strategic asset allocation. Strategic asset allocation establishes the benchmark allocation among the major asset classes for the long-term investment process. Strategic asset allocation is concerned with optimizing the risk-return trade-off of long-term asset allocation given the specific objectives of an individual or an organization. Depending on the type of institutional investor, the benchmark is typically reviewed on a quarterly, one year, or up to five year basis. The oversight committee decides on the range of possible deviations of the tactical asset allocation from the strategic benchmark and sets a tactical risk budget. The extend can be restricted in terms of (ex ante) tracking error, portfolio beta, or (ex ante) value at risk. The second tier, an investment committee, decides on deviations from the strategic benchmark within the given tactical risk budget.

One key difference between strategic and tactical asset allocation is the time horizon of investment decisions. Tactical asset allocation is applied routinely as part of continuing asset management. The purpose of tactical asset allocation is adding value to the strategic allocation by increasing the investment return or reducing portfolio risk. Another difference is that tactical asset allocation is benchmark-relative portfolio selection with self-financing weight reallocations. Underweighting and overweighting of assets or asset classes aims at outperforming the strategic benchmark. Active strategies of the portfolio mandates can add additional sources of return and risk diversification. Placing the same active bet in several markets reduces market-specific risks. A wide breadth of alpha sources reduces the dependence of widening and narrowing market inefficiencies.

Several empirical studies investigate the impact of strategic asset allocation and active management on portfolio performance. Concerning the variability of *returns across time*, Brinson, Hood, and Beebower (1986), Brinson, Singer, and Beebower (1991), and Ibbotson and Kaplan (2000) find that return variability is explained with an R^2 of approximately 90 % by the variability of the policy returns, i.e. returns of the strategic benchmark. However, this does not imply little opportunity to add value through active management; differences between performances of two funds can also be a result of differing strategic policies. Concerning the variation of *return differences among funds*, approximately 40 % of the return difference among funds is explained by policy differences, according to Ibbotson and Kaplan (2000). The relatively low R^2 of 40 % shows that a large amount of variability must stem from active management. In total, while the strategic asset allocation is important for determining the overall level of returns, successfull active management can essentially distinguish between funds with similar strategic asset allocations. However, since the costs of active management reduces the portfolio performance, the average active manager must be underperforming the market on a cost-adjusted basis.[5] Therefore, it is essential for the success of active managed portfolios to have the ability to select superior managers in order to earn above-average returns.

Besides strategic asset allocation, another instrument for controlling the long-term implementation of the institution's objectives is risk budgeting. The aim of risk allocation is to give the right amount of flexibility to delegated investment decisions. A three layer set-up implies three distinct sources of risk and return. Risk budgets are relevant on each tier:

- Strategic risk budgets are the risks amounts inherent in the strategic asset allocation of wealth to each individual asset class. Reverse

[5]The majority of empirical studies find that, on average, active management fails to outperform passive benchmark portfolios and in many cases underperforms passive indices even before expenses, see e.g. Malkiel (1995), Carhart (1997). Wermers (2000) finds that funds hold stocks that outperform the market, but their net returns underperform the market due to expenses and transaction costs.

optimization using the classical model of Markowitz (1952) can be used to calculate the implied risk budget that each asset contributes to total portfolio risk.[6]

- The tactical risk budget restricts the tactical deviations from the strategic benchmark portfolio. The oversight committee decides on the optimal tactical risk budget that is assigned to the members of the investment committee.

- Active risk is risk introduced through active strategies at the portfolio level as well as within asset classes. Active risk budgets are assigned individually to portfolio managers based on their investment skills.

There is little experience with the performance of active management for alternative risk budgets. However, expectations of the effectiveness of active management are necessary when placing active portfolio mandates and allocating tactical and active risk budgets. The following section presents a model for the tactical risk allocation decision of the investment committee when the strategic asset allocation is already completed. The models presented in chapter 7 address the oversight committee's problem of the simultaneous strategic asset allocation and active risk allocation.

4.3 The Model Framework

This section introduces the safety first approach for an investor who delegates portfolio selection to an active portfolio manager. The principal defines a strategic benchmark and delegates portfolio selection to an agent. Depending on the set of available risk constraints, the principal's task is to provide constraints on tracking error and eventually portfolio beta. The

[6]See also page 17 for the calculation of the asset's implied risk budgets.

agent is supposed to choose reallocations of benchmark within set risk limits. The model represents the principal's problem of allocating a tactical or active risk budget to one agent as well as the agent's benchmark-relative portfolio selection. The model can represent the relation between a private client and institutional investor as well as a two-tier organizational set-up of a managed fund.

The principal-agent model is based on standard assumptions of neoclassical finance as given by assumptions 2.1 (frictionless market) and 2.2 (risky assets) in chapter 2. Throughout this chapter, the principal is loss avers and aims at minimizing the probability $P(R_P < \tau)$ of falling short a fixed threshold return τ, $\tau < \mu_{\text{MVP}}$, as stated by assumption 2.3' (Roy criterion). By assumption 2.4, the asset returns are assumed to be normally distributed. She specifies a strategic benchmark $\mathbf{x}_B$ and hires an agent for benchmark-relative portfolio selection. His remuneration is based on benchmark excess return and therefore he wants to maximize the expected benchmark excess return $E[R_P - R_B]$ as stated in assumption 3.1'. There is no contract available that enables the principal to provide incentives to reduce the shortfall probability. The benchmark that should be outperformed is supposed to be given and have expected return μ_B with $\mu_B > \mu_{\text{MVP}}$.

The principal-agent model deviates from the neoclassical finance theory with respect to an information asymmetry assumption. Due to lack of information or limited capacity on decision making, investment decisions are delegated to an agent. Agency costs with respect to the portfolio manager's compensation are assumed to be negligible in the principals utility for simplicity – except for the last section 4.8 of this chapter. Instead, we focus on the principal's possibilities to control the portfolio selection using risk constraints on tracking error and eventually portfolio beta. Whether she is able to determine optimal constraints, depends on her available information about the financial market. The subsequent sections reveal that the following levels of information should be distinguished. The information levels are further discussed in section 4.7.

Assumption 4.1 (Information Asymmetry).
The agent knows the expected return $\boldsymbol{\mu}$ of all assets and the covariance $\boldsymbol{V}$ of their returns. The principal has one of the following levels of information:

(a) *no information:* $\{\}$,

(b) *mean and volatility of returns of TEV portfolios and mean return of MVP:* $\{\mu_B, \sigma_B, \mu_{\text{MVP}}, d\}$,

(c) *mean and volatility of returns of frontier and TEV portfolios:* $\{\mu_B, \sigma_B, \boldsymbol{A}\}$, or

(d) *complete information on expected return and covariance of returns of all assets:* $\{\boldsymbol{\mu}, \boldsymbol{V}\}$.

Sections 4.4 – 4.6 below show how the principal can specify optimal constraints given an intermediate level of information. Using risk constraints, the principal may control the risk and return properties of the portfolio chosen by the manager. The following assumption provides the set of portfolio constraints that the principal can choose from.

Assumption 4.2 (Principal's Control Variables).
The principal chooses to restrict the delegated portfolio selection process via one of the following sets of portfolio constraints:

(a) *tracking error σ_s only,*

(b) *tracking error σ_s when portfolio beta $\beta_{P,B}$ is a fixed standard value, e.g. $\beta_{P,B} = 1$,*

(c) *tracking error σ_s and portfolio beta $\beta_{P,B}$.*

Principal and agent enter into a contract that induces the agent to maximize benchmark excess return and gives the principal the choice of certain risk constraints to control portfolio selection. This framework explicitly models the principal's decision problem to choose type and value of constraints. In this way, the framework also addresses the problem of the optimal governance of the portfolio delegation.

4.4 Minimizing Shortfall Probability for TEV Portfolios

This section shows how investors can pursue the safety first approach when delegating portfolio selection to benchmark outperforming agents.[7] Given only a tracking error constraint and performance depending salary, portfolio managers are eager to maximize the benchmark excess return. Section 3.1 shows that they compose TEV portfolios. Investors who delegate portfolio selection to portfolio managers might anticipate such a kind of portfolio selection. Investors can use the benchmark tracking error constraint σ_s as a tool to control portfolio selection. The threshold shortfall probability of the TEV portfolio can be reduced in case that the tracking error constraint is chosen properly. Figure 4.2 illustrates this principal-agent problem. The corresponding problem for the investor to solve is

[7]While this section investigates the safety first approach for *absolute* returns of benchmark-oriented portfolios, the safety first approach has also been applied to benchmark *excess* returns: Reichling (1996, p. 40 et seq.) minimizes the probability $P(R_P - R_B < \tau)$ of the benchmark excess return falling short a threshold return.

Problem 4.1 (Safety First for TEV Portfolios).
Determine the tracking error constraint such that the probability of the TEV portfolio falling short the threshold return τ is minimized:

objective: $\min_{\sigma_s} P(R_P < \tau)$

constraint: $\boldsymbol{s}$ *is solution of the TEV problem 3.1(2) with constraint* σ_s^2 .

Proposition 4.2 (TEV Portfolio with Minimum Shortfall Probability).
The minimum threshold shortfall probability in the benchmark-relative portfolio selection problem 3.1(2), i.e. the solution of problem 4.1, can be achieved with tracking error volatility

$$\sigma_s = \frac{1}{\sqrt{d}} \frac{d\sigma_B^2 - (\mu_B - \tau)(\mu_B - \mu_{\text{MVP}})}{\mu_{\text{MVP}} - \tau} . \tag{4.1}$$

With this tracking error volatility, the expected excess return is

$$\boldsymbol{\mu}'\boldsymbol{s} = \sqrt{d}\sigma_s = \frac{d\sigma_B^2 - (\mu_B - \tau)(\mu_B - \mu_{\text{MVP}})}{\mu_{\text{MVP}} - \tau} .$$

Proof. Section 2.3 shows that the minimum shortfall probability for a given threshold return τ can be obtained by maximizing the slope $(\mu_P - \tau)/\sigma_P$ of the shortfall line. For TEV portfolios, the slope

$$\frac{\mu_P - \tau}{\sigma_P} = \frac{\mu_B + \sqrt{d}\sigma_s - \tau}{\sqrt{\sigma_B^2 + \frac{2}{\sqrt{d}}(\mu_B - \mu_{\text{MVP}})\sigma_s + \sigma_s^2}}$$

can be calculated with the expected return and variance of return from equations (3.2) and (3.3). It is a function of σ_s. The maximum satisfies the condition

$$\frac{\partial \frac{\mu_P - \tau}{\sigma_P}}{\partial \sigma_s} = \frac{\sqrt{d}\sigma_P - \frac{1}{2\sigma_P}\left(\frac{2}{\sqrt{d}}(\mu_B - \mu_{\text{MVP}}) + 2\sigma_s\right)\left(\mu_B + \sqrt{d}\sigma_s - \tau\right)}{\sigma_P^2} = 0 .$$

After replacing σ_P as given in equation (3.3), one can solve for σ_s. This equation has two solutions. With assumption $\tau < \mu_{\text{MVP}} < \mu_B$, the maximum is given by equation (4.1). □

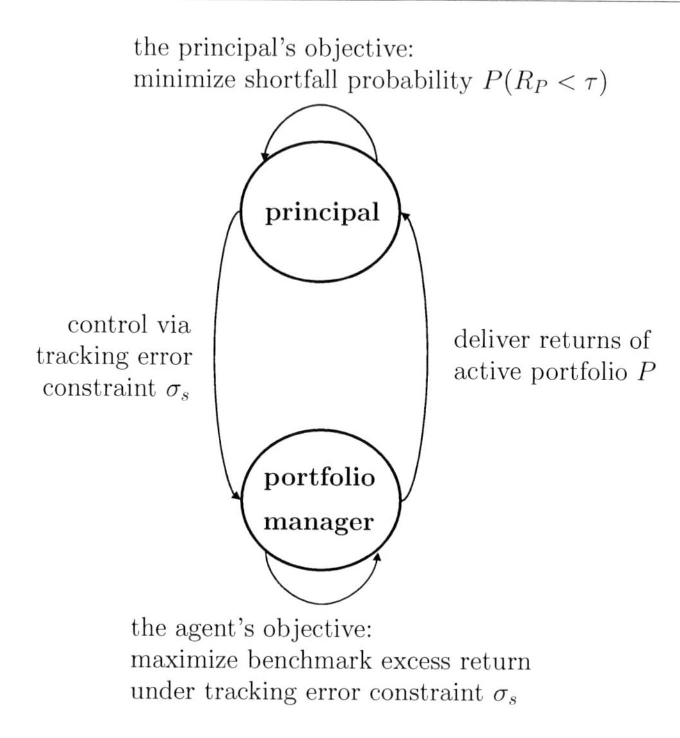

Figure 4.2: Principal Controls the Agent's Portfolio Selection via Tracking Error Constraint

Figure 4.3 illustrates the TEV portfolio with minimum shortfall probability of proposition 4.2. The investor can reduce the benchmark's threshold shortfall probability by delegating portfolio selection to a TEV portfolio composing manager. In this way, the investor profits from delegating, since she is not able to compose such a shortfall probability reducing portfolio herself. Proposition 4.2 shows how the investor specifies the tracking error constraints optimally. Since the optimal tracking error increases with σ_B and decreases with μ_B, the optimal risk budget increases with benchmark inefficiency. In other words, the more efficient the benchmark is, the tighter the optimal tracking error constraints are.

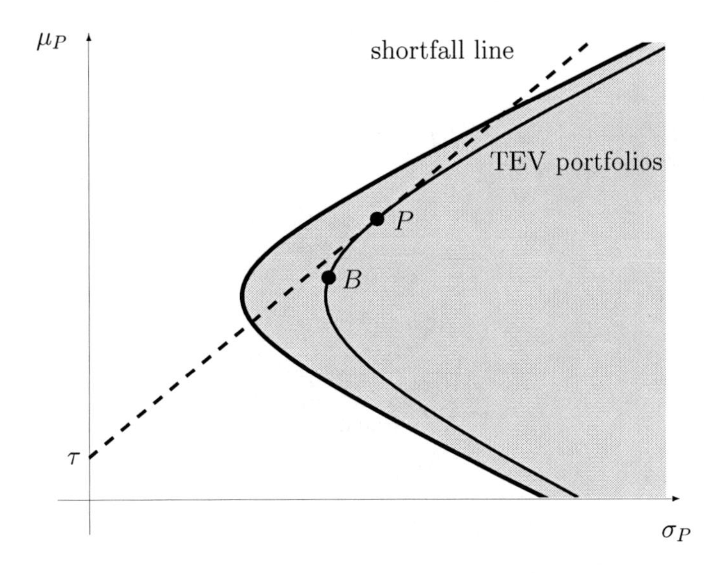

Figure 4.3: TEV Portfolio P with Minimum Shortfall Probability

4.5 Minimizing Shortfall Probability for TEVBR Portfolios

The systematic risk of a portfolio P with respect to a benchmark portfolio B can be measured with portfolio beta $\beta_{P,B} \equiv \sigma_{P,B}/\sigma_B^2$. The portfolio beta is often restricted to a standard value close to 1. This section derives the optimal tracking error budget such that the agent's benchmark-relative portfolio selection minimizes the threshold shortfall probability given a fixed standard beta constraint. This principal-agent problem and its solution are illustrated in figures 4.4 and 4.5, respectively. As in the previous section, the principal's only variable to control the portfolio selection is the tracking error constraint.

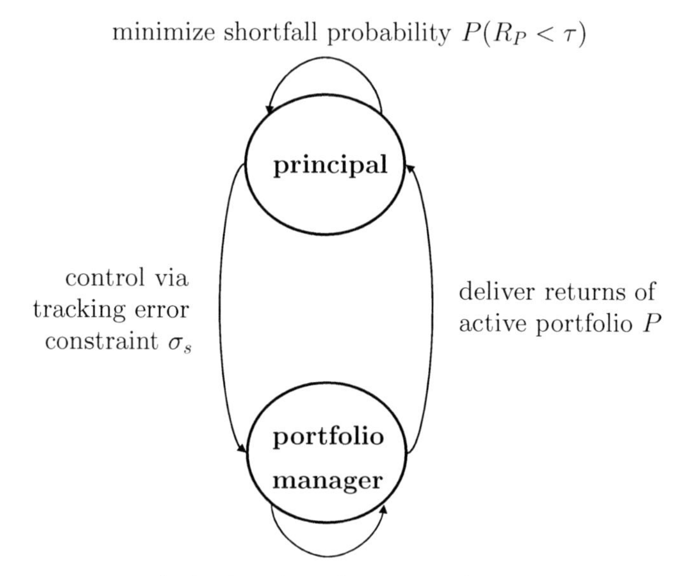

Figure 4.4: Principal Controls Beta-Restricted Portfolio Selection via Tracking Error Constraint

Problem 4.3 (Safety First for TEVBR Portfolios with Given Beta).
For a given beta constraint, determine the optimal tracking error constraint such that the probability of the TEVBR portfolio falling short a threshold return is minimized:

$$\begin{aligned} &\textit{objective:} && \min_{\sigma_s} \; P(R_P < \tau) \\ &\textit{constraint:} && \boldsymbol{s} \textit{ is a solution of the TEVBR problem 3.3(2)} \\ & && \textit{with constraint } \sigma_s \textit{ and fixed } \beta_{P,B} \, . \end{aligned}$$

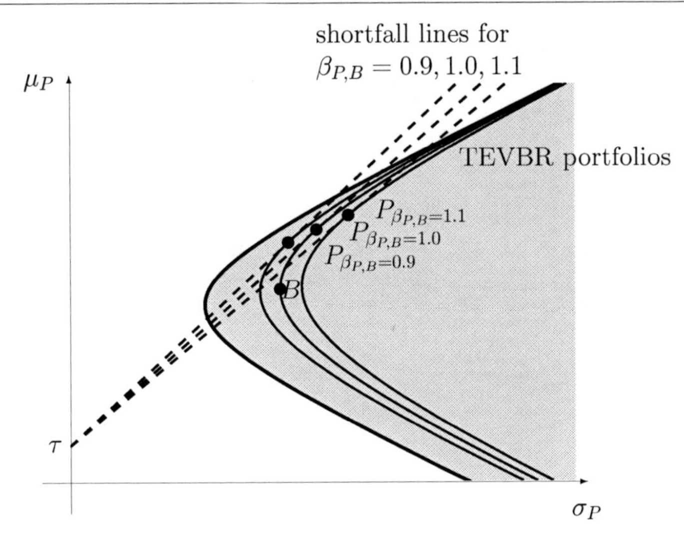

Figure 4.5: TEVBR Portfolios with Minimum Shortfall Probability

Proposition 4.4 (Minimum Shortfall TEVBR Portfolio for Given Beta). *The minimum threshold shortfall probability in problem 3.3(2) with fixed beta factor, i.e. the solution of problem 4.3, can be achieved with tracking error constraint*

$$\sigma_s = \frac{\sigma_B^2}{\sqrt{\sigma_B^2 - \sigma_{\mathrm{MVP}}^2}} \cdot \sqrt{(\beta_{P,B} - 1)^2 + \frac{\sigma_{\mathrm{MVP}}^2 \det \boldsymbol{H}((1 - 2\beta_{P,B})\sigma_{\mathrm{MVP}}^2 + \beta_{P,B}^2\sigma_B^2)^2}{((\mu_B - \tau)(\sigma_B^2 - \sigma_{\mathrm{MVP}}^2) + (\beta_{P,B} - 1)(\mu_B - \mu_{\mathrm{MVP}})\sigma_B^2)^2}} \,. \tag{4.2}$$

Given this tracking error volatility, the expected excess return is

$$\boldsymbol{\mu}'\boldsymbol{s} = \frac{(a - b\mu_B - b\tau + c\mu_B\tau)(1 - \beta_{P,B}) - (a - 2b\mu_B + c\mu_B^2)\beta_{P,B} + (ac - b^2)\sigma_B^2\beta_{P,B}^2}{(\mu_B - \tau)(\sigma_B^2 - \frac{1}{c}) + (\mu_B - \frac{b}{c})(\beta_{P,B} - 1)\sigma_B^2} \frac{\sigma_B^2}{c} \tag{4.3}$$

$$= d \frac{\sigma_{P_B^*,P_\tau^*}(1 - \beta_{P,B}) - (\sigma_{P_B^*}^2 - \sigma_B^2\beta_{P,B})\beta_{P,B}}{\mu_{\mathrm{MVP}} - \tau - (\mu_B - \tau)\frac{\sigma_{\mathrm{MVP}}^2}{\sigma_B^2} + (\mu_B - \mu_{\mathrm{MVP}})\beta_{P,B}} \,,$$

where P_B^* and P_τ^* are frontier portfolios with expected return μ_B and τ, respectively.

Proof. We want to maximize the slope $(\mu_P - \tau)/\sigma_P$ of the active portfolio solution of the TEVBR problem 3.3(2). It is a function of the tracking error volatility

$$\frac{\mu_P - \tau}{\sigma_P} = \frac{\mu_B + G - \tau}{\sqrt{\sigma_s^2 + (2\beta_{P,B} - 1)\sigma_B^2}},$$

where the expected excess return G and the variance of return of the active portfolio σ_P^2 are given by equations (3.11) and (3.10). The maximum slope satisfies the condition

$$\frac{\partial \frac{\mu_P - \tau}{\sigma_P}}{\partial \sigma_s} = \frac{\frac{\partial G}{\partial \sigma_s}\sigma_P - \frac{1}{2\sigma_P} 2\sigma_s(\mu_B + G - \tau)}{\sigma_P^2} = 0$$

which is equivalent to

$$\begin{aligned} 0 &= \frac{\partial G}{\partial \sigma_s} \cdot \sigma_P^2 - \sigma_s(\mu_B + G - \tau) \\ &= \sigma_s \frac{\sqrt{\det \boldsymbol{H}}(\sigma_s^2 + (2\beta_{P,B} - 1)\sigma_B^2)}{\sqrt{-c(-1 + \beta_{P,B})^2\sigma_B^4 + (-1 + c\sigma_B^2)\sigma_s^2}} - \sigma_s(\mu_B + G - \tau) \,. \end{aligned}$$

After replacing G as given by equation (3.11), one can solve for σ_s. Solution candidates are $\sigma_s = 0$ and the maximum given by equation (4.2). The provided representation for σ_s follows from equations (2.7) and (2.8) of expected return and variance of return of the minimum variance portfolio.

The expected excess return for general $\beta_{P,B}$ and minimum shortfall probability can be obtained by inserting the tracking error volatility from equation (4.2) in equation (3.11) and rearranging with help of equations (3.7) and (2.13). □

4.6 Minimizing Shortfall Probability with Efficient TEVBR Portfolios

This section shows that delegated investing can also yield efficient frontier portfolios. Therefore, the principal has to control portfolio selection via tracking error and beta constraint, as is illustrated in figure 4.6. Given optimal specified constraints, the portfolio manager composes an efficient frontier portfolio.

Problem 4.5 (Safety First for TEVBR Portfolios).
Determine the optimal beta and tracking error constraints such that the solution of the TEVBR problem 3.3(2) minimizes the threshold shortfall probability:

$$\begin{aligned} &\textit{objective:} && \min_{\beta_{P,B},\sigma_s} \; P(R_P < \tau) \\ &\textit{constraint:} && \boldsymbol{s} \textit{ is a solution of the TEVBR problem 3.3(2)} \\ & && \textit{with constraints } \beta_{P,B} \textit{ and } \sigma_s \,. \end{aligned}$$

The first-best solution of the safety first problem is an efficient frontier portfolio with benchmark excess return $\overline{G} \equiv (a - b\tau)/(b - c\tau) - \mu_B$ according to proposition 2.6. This portfolio can also be achieved with a TEVBR portfolio as a solution of above problem 4.5 if portfolio constraints are chosen optimally. Hence, second-best solution and first-best solution coincide.

Proposition 4.6 (Efficient TEVBR Portfolio with Min. Shortfall Prob.).
The minimum shortfall probability portfolio is an efficient frontier portfolio with expected excess return $\overline{G} \equiv (a - b\tau)/(b - c\tau) - \mu_B$. It is the solution of the TEVBR problem 3.3(2) with beta constraint

$$\begin{aligned} \beta_{P,B} &= \frac{a - 2b\mu_B + c\mu_B^2 + (c\mu_B - b)\overline{G}}{(ac - b^2)\sigma_B^2} = \frac{\sigma_{B*}^2}{\sigma_B^2} + \frac{\mu_B - \mu_{\text{MVP}}}{d\sigma_B^2}\overline{G} \\ &= \frac{(\mu_B - \tau)\sigma_{\text{MVP}}^2}{(\mu_{\text{MVP}} - \tau)\sigma_B^2} \end{aligned}$$

and tracking error variance constraint

$$\begin{aligned}\sigma_s^2 &= \sigma_B^2 - \frac{a - 2b\mu_B + c\mu_B^2 - c\overline{G}^2}{ac - b^2} = \sigma_B^2 - \sigma_{B^*}^2 + \frac{\overline{G}^2}{d} \\ &= \frac{a - 2b\mu_B + 2c\mu_B\tau - c\tau^2 + \sigma_B^2(b^2 - 2bc\tau + c^2\tau^2)}{(b - c\tau)^2},\end{aligned}$$

where B^* denotes a frontier portfolio with expected return μ_B.

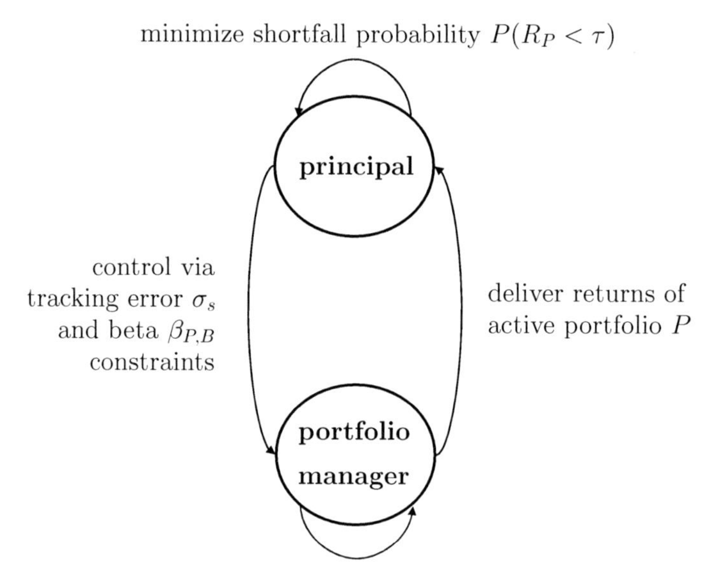

Figure 4.6: Principal Controls Portfolio Selection via Tracking Error and Beta Constraints

Proof. Proposition 2.6 shows that the first-best solution of the safety first problem is an efficient frontier portfolio with expected return

$$\mu_P = \mu_B + \overline{G} = \frac{a - b\tau}{b - c\tau} .$$

According to proposition 3.5, this frontier portfolio is also solution of the TEVBR problem 3.3(2) if constraints are set to

$$\begin{aligned}
\beta_{P,B} &= \frac{a - 2b\mu_B + c\mu_B^2 + (c\mu_B - b)\overline{G}}{(ac - b^2)\sigma_B^2} = \frac{\mu_B - \tau}{(b - c\tau)\sigma_B^2} = \frac{(\mu_B - \tau)\sigma_{\text{MVP}}^2}{(\mu_{\text{MVP}} - \tau)\sigma_B^2} \\
\sigma_s^2 &= \sigma_B^2 - \frac{a - 2b\mu_B + c\mu_B^2 - c\overline{G}^2}{ac - b^2} \\
&= \frac{a - 2b\mu_B + 2c\mu_B\tau - c\tau^2 + \sigma_B^2(b^2 - 2bc\tau + c^2\tau^2)}{(b - c\tau)^2} ,
\end{aligned}$$

where the excess return is replaced using $\overline{G} = \mu_B - (a - b\tau)/(b - c\tau)$. The following alternative representation of the tracking error constraint is not mentioned in the proposition:

$$\begin{aligned}
\sigma_s^2 &= \sigma_B^2 + \frac{(a/c - \tau^2)}{(b/c - \tau)^2 c} - \frac{2\mu_B}{(b/c - \tau)c} \\
&= \sigma_B^2 + \frac{(\mu_{P*}^2 - \tau^2)\sigma_{\text{MVP}}^2}{(\mu_{\text{MVP}} - \tau)^2} - \frac{2\mu_B\sigma_{\text{MVP}}^2}{(\mu_{\text{MVP}} - \tau)} ,
\end{aligned}$$

where $\mu_P^* = \sqrt{a}/\sqrt{c}$ is the expected return of the frontier portfolio P^* with maximum mean-variance ratio as specified in table 2.2. □

Figure 4.7 illustrates TEVBR portfolios when beta is chosen optimally. They are very close to the efficient frontier. If the tracking error constraint is also optimal, the portfolio manager composes a TEVBR portfolio that is mean-variance efficient and minimizes the threshold shortfall probability. In this case, the second-best solution coincides with the first-best solution. Proposition 4.6 can additionally be used for generating benchmark dominating portfolios, i.e. portfolios with higher expected return and less total risk than the benchmark. For this purpose, the threshold return has to be within specific bounds that are derived in the appendix.

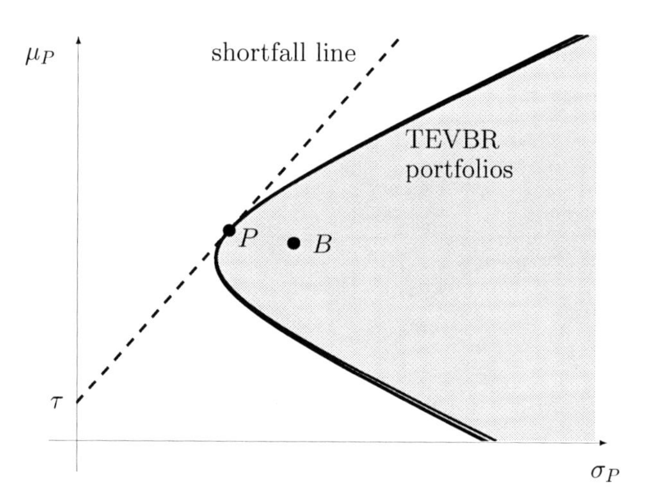

Figure 4.7: Mean-Variance Efficient TEVBR Portfolio P with Minimum Shortfall Probability

4.7 Information Level and Type of Delegation

Investment decisions are often delegated due to lack of information on financial markets. This section discusses the information aspect of the presented principal-agent model. It identifies the necessary information that enables the principal to make optimal delegation decisions. Furthermore, it shows that the agent does not need to disclose his knowledge of all assets' mean returns and covariances, but to communicate some properties of the information matrix. In our model, the investor is able to choose the type of constraints and to set them optimally if she has appropriate financial information.

Calculating the optimal risk constraints is based on knowing the input parameters of the formulas derived in the previous three sections. By inspecting these formulas, four essential information levels can be differentiated and they were already introduced in assumption 4.1 (information asymmetry). Without any information, the investor still can delegate portfolio management, but she cannot be sure whether her objective is satisfied better than with an investment in the benchmark portfolio. Without information asymmetry as given by assumption 4.1(d), no delegation would be needed. The investor could compose the first-best portfolio that is presented in section 2.3. The remaining two information levels are intermediary levels with increasing information:

$$\{\ \} \subset \{\mu_B, \sigma_B, \mu_{\text{MVP}}, d\} \subset \{\mu_B, \sigma_B, \boldsymbol{A}\} \subset \{\boldsymbol{\mu}, \boldsymbol{V}\}\ .$$

In case of partial information as given by assumptions 4.1(b) and 4.1(c), the principal can use equations (3.2) and (3.3) to determine the mean and variance of return of the TEV portfolio that the agent composes if given only a tracking error constraint. The partial information of assumption 4.1(c) allows the principal to additionally calculate the mean and variance of return of frontier portfolios.

Table 4.1 shows the type of delegated investing that the principal should choose depending on her level of information and available set of constraints.[8] With no information at all, she might choose a random portfolio or a benchmark portfolio. If she delegates, she cannot be sure that the managed portfolio is better than the benchmark. If she knows the value of the variables of formulas for the optimal constraints, she can choose a TEV or a TEVBR portfolio composing manager and set constraints optimally. Knowing $\{\mu_B, \sigma_B, \mu_{\text{MVP}}, d\}$, she can specify optimal constraints for TEV

[8]This decision problem addresses the governance of the delegation process. Williamson (2000) specifies four levels in which theories on institutions, also called the new institutional economics, can be classified in. The principal's optimization of the constraint values and the agent's portfolio selection occurs on level 4, called "neoclassical economics/agency theory", where the purpose is to get the marginal conditions right. The framework for choosing the type of constraints, tracking error only or tracking error and portfolio beta constraint, occurs on level 3 "transaction costs economics" which is concerned with getting the governance structures and contracts right.

second-best solution	control instruments available to principal		
	σ_s	σ_s or $\{\sigma_s, \beta_{P,B} = 1\}$	σ_s or $\{\sigma_s, \beta_{P,B}\}$
principal's level of information			
$\{\mu_B, \sigma_B, \mu_{\text{MVP}}, d\}$	TEV	TEV	TEV
$\{\mu_B, \sigma_B, \boldsymbol{A}\}$	TEV	TEV or TEVBR	TEVBR[9]
$\{\boldsymbol{\mu}, \boldsymbol{V}\}$	no delegation necessary	no delegation necessary	no delegation necessary

Table 4.1: Type of Second-Best Solution for Given Information Level and Set of Available Risk Constraints

portfolios. With complete information on expected return and variance of frontier portfolios as given by information matrix $\boldsymbol{A}$, she still would not be able to compose frontier portfolios. However, she is able to specify the constraints on TEVBR portfolios such that a manager would compose the first-best solution, a frontier portfolio, for her. If she knows $\boldsymbol{A}$, but can add only a standard beta constraint as given by assumption 4.2(b), she has to choose between a TEV and a TEVBR portfolio. It is best to calculate shortfall probabilities of TEV and TEVBR portfolio and choose accordingly. With all information, $\{\boldsymbol{\mu}, \boldsymbol{V}\}$, there would be no need of delegation, since the investor could compose frontier portfolios herself.

One might argue that investors usually may not have sufficient information at all to choose any constraints optimally. The optimal tracking error constraint of the TEV problem is a function $\sigma_s = \sigma_s(\mu_B, \sigma_B, \mu_{\text{MVP}}, d)$. The manager can reveal μ_B, σ_B, μ_{MVP}, and d without the delegation becoming

[9]With optimal chosen constraints σ_s and $\beta_{P,B}$, the resulting second-best solution, a TEVBR portfolio, coincides with the first-best solution.

dispensable, since he does not need to disclose his knowledge on expected returns and covariance of returns of all assets.[10] The principal could also research these variables on her own. The model shows that adapting the tracking error constraint is necessary if the shape of the mean-variance frontier changes fundamentally. The investor does not need to care about changes of single securities' expected returns and covariances. In this way, the model incorporates a typical feature of condensing information in the delegation process.

4.8 Optimization with Management Fee

The agent's remuneration has been neglected so far in the delegation process. This section shows how a stylized contract can be specified to induce the manager to choose the optimal active return and risk combination of the second-best solution. Second, we derive the optimal active risk budget given that a management fee reduces the portfolio return.

We consider a manager employment contract that puts incentives to generate active return and disincentives on active risk. While performance dependent compensation is usually based on ex post observations of portfolio return, the manager composes the portfolio based on ex ante beliefs. The expected compensation is introduced as a rate f of total portfolio value that depends on the ex ante active return μ_s and active risk σ_s:

$$f(\mu_s, \sigma_s) \equiv c_0 + c_1\mu_s - c_2\sigma_s^2 = c_0 + c_1\left(\mu_s - \frac{c_2}{c_1}\sigma_s^2\right)$$

with positive constants c_1, c_2 and fixed compensation c_0. The fixed compensation element c_0 is a component added to the contract considered

[10]Some models implicitly assume that the agents disclose a substantial part of their private information. In the work of van Binsbergen, Brandt, and Koijen (2007, p. 10), the principal needs to know the assets' expected returns and their covariances with the delegated portfolios.

in Cornell and Roll (2005). While the principal's net return is reduced by the management fee, the agent maximizes his expected compensation based on returns before deduction of expenses. This contract induces the agent to compose TEV portfolios that are presented in section 3.1. Given a fixed amount of active risk σ_s, the portfolio manager composes TEV portfolios with $\mu_s = \sqrt{d}\sigma_s$ and his expected compensation is $f(\sqrt{d}\sigma_s, \sigma_s) = c_0 + c_1\sqrt{d}\sigma_s - c_2\sigma_s^2$. The principal can set the constants c_1 and c_2 such that the agent chooses the optimal active risk and return of proposition 4.2. The first order condition on the agent's maximum compensation

$$\frac{\partial f}{\partial \sigma_s} = c_1\sqrt{d} - 2c_2\sigma_s = 0$$

and the second order condition $\partial^2 f/\partial\sigma_s^2 = -2c_2 < 0$ yield the optimal ratio

$$\frac{c_2}{c_1} = \frac{\sqrt{d}}{2\sigma_s} = \frac{d}{2\mu_s}, \tag{4.4}$$

where μ_s and σ_s are given in proposition 4.2. Holding this ratio fixed, the value of c_1 or c_2 as well as the fixed compensation rate c_0 can be negotiated arbitrarly by principal and agent.

In the following, we show how the principal can account for that the management fee reduces the portfolio return. The expected portfolio return after management costs is $\mu_P - f(\mu_s, \sigma_s)$. Although the portfolio manager's salary depends on ex post realizations of portfolio return, the active portfolio composition and the negotiation of the compensation contract are based on ex ante expectations. The design of the optimal contract should take into consideration that the management fee reduces the portfolio return. The procedure of contract negotiation might be structured in four steps: In the first step, principal and agent agree on a total expected fee $\widehat{f}$ and to restrict tracking error only.

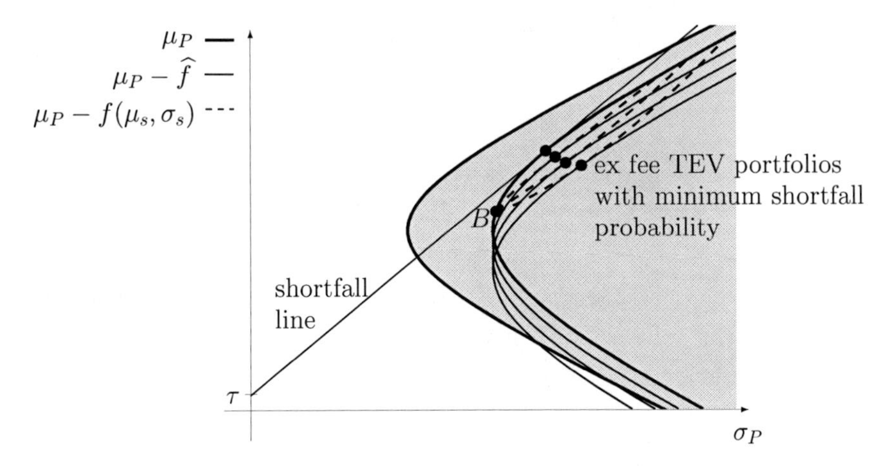

Figure 4.8: Ex Management Fee TEV Portfolios with Minimum Shortfall Probability

As a second step, the principal determines the optimal active risk of the minimum shortfall portfolio among all TEV portfolios after reduction of the management fee. Figure 4.8 illustrates TEV portfolios in (μ, σ)-space with and without reduction of management fees as well as TEV portfolios with minimum shortfall probability of ex fee returns. Since minimizing the shortfall probability of ex fee returns is equivalent to maximizing the ratio

$$\frac{\mu_{P,\text{ex fee}} - \tau}{\sigma_{P,\text{ex fee}}} = \frac{\mu_P - \widehat{f} - \tau}{\sigma_P},$$

the first order condition for the maximum of the ratio yields the optimal active risk

$$\widehat{\sigma}_s = \frac{d\sigma_B^2 - (\mu_B - \mu_{\text{MVP}})\left(\mu_B - \widehat{f} - \tau\right)}{\sqrt{d}\left(\mu_{\text{MVP}} - \widehat{f} - \tau\right)}$$

which also results from proposition 4.2 with threshold return $\tau + \widehat{f}$.

In a third step, the optimal ratio

$$\frac{c_2}{c_1} = \frac{\sqrt{d}}{2\widehat{\sigma}_s} = \frac{1}{2} \frac{d\left(\mu_{\mathrm{MVP}} - \widehat{f} - \tau\right)}{d\sigma_B^2 - (\mu_B - \mu_{\mathrm{MVP}})(\mu_B - \widehat{f} - \tau)}$$

needs to be fixed in contract negotiation to achieve the optimal amount of active risk and return. In the last step, the fixed compensation rate c_0 and the constant c_1 are adjusted in order to satisfy $c_0 + c_1(\widehat{\mu}_s - \widehat{\sigma}_s^2 c_2^*/c_1^*) = \widehat{f}$, e.g. by setting $c_0 = 0$ and $c_1 = \frac{\widehat{f}}{\widehat{\mu}_s - \widehat{\sigma}_s^2 c_2^*/c_1^*}$. If the portfolio manager chooses active risk different from $\widehat{\sigma}_s$, his expected compensation rate will be less than $\widehat{f}$. This could even improve the ex fee portfolio performance as is indicated by the dashed lines in figure 4.8.

Appendix

This appendix derives bounds on the threshold return and on the active risk for which the safety first approach yields benchmark dominating frontier portfolios. These bounds are valid for all problems with efficient portfolios as solution. Hence they can also be used to ensure that the solution is not only efficient but also benchmark dominating, e.g. for the TEVBR problem discussed in section 4.6.

Suppose we are trying to obtain benchmark dominating portfolios with the safety first approach. How should the threshold return be specified in this case? Figure 4.9 illustrates lower and upper bounds on threshold returns, τ^* and $\widehat{\tau}$, for which problem 2.5 has a benchmark dominating solution. The smaller the distance of benchmark and efficient frontier, the tighter the bounds on the optimal threshold return are.

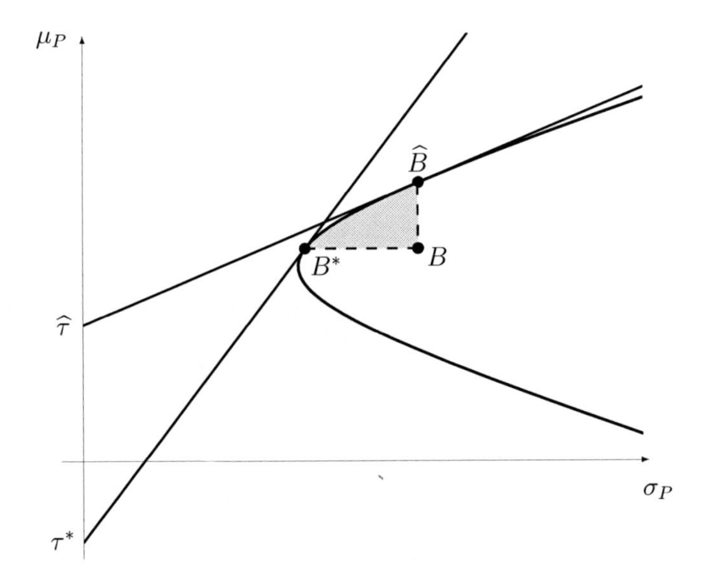

Figure 4.9: Bounds on Threshold Return and Shortfall Lines

Proposition 4.7 (Bounds on Threshold for Dominating Frontier Ptfs.).
Let B denote a benchmark with expected return μ_B, $\mu_B > \mu_{\text{MVP}}$, and variance of return σ_B^2. The solution of the safety first problem 2.5 dominates benchmark B if and only if the threshold return satisfies

$$\frac{a - b\mu_B}{b - c\mu_B} \leq \tau \leq \mu_{\text{MVP}} - \frac{\sqrt{d}\,\sigma_{\text{MVP}}^2}{\sqrt{\sigma_B^2 - \sigma_{\text{MVP}}^2}}\,.$$

Proof. Proposition 2.6 shows that the solution of the safety first problem 2.5 is an efficient frontier portfolio. A frontier portfolio dominates the benchmark B if it is a convex combination of the frontier portfolios B^* and $\widehat{B}$ as illustrated in figure 4.9. Portfolio B^* has expected return μ_B and has minimum shortfall probability for the threshold return $\tau^* = (a - b\mu_B)/(b - c\mu_B)$ according to proposition 2.6. Frontier portfolio $\widehat{B}$ has variance of return $\sigma_{\widehat{B}}^2 = \sigma_B^2$ and equation (2.2) yields its expected return $\mu_{\widehat{B}} = b/c + \sqrt{(a - b^2/c)(\sigma_B^2 - 1/c)}$ using $\mu_{\widehat{B}} > \mu_{\text{MVP}} = b/c$. Proposition 2.6 yields the corresponding threshold returns

$$\widehat{\tau} = \frac{b}{c} - \frac{1}{c}\sqrt{\frac{a - b^2/c}{\sigma_B^2 - 1/c}} = \mu_{\text{MVP}} - \frac{\sqrt{d}\,\sigma_{\text{MVP}}^2}{\sqrt{\sigma_B^2 - \sigma_{\text{MVP}}^2}}\,.$$

□

Whether an efficient portfolio dominates the benchmark, can also be verified with its tracking error. The following proposition presents bounds on the active risk and the optimal amount of active risk for a given threshold return.

Proposition 4.8 (Bounds on Active Risk for Dominating Frontier Ptfs.).
Let $\mu_B > \mu_{\text{MVP}}$. A frontier portfolio P dominates a benchmark B with expected return μ_B if and only if its tracking error variance satisfies

$$\begin{aligned}
&\sigma_B^2 - \sigma_{\text{MVP}}^2 - \frac{1}{d}\left(\mu_B - \mu_{\text{MVP}}\right)^2 \\
&\leq \sigma_s^2 \leq 2\left(\sigma_B^2 - \sigma_{\text{MVP}}^2\right) - \frac{2}{\sqrt{d}}\sqrt{\sigma_B^2 - \sigma_{\text{MVP}}^2}\,\left(\mu_B - \mu_{\text{MVP}}\right).
\end{aligned}$$

For given threshold return τ, $\tau < \mu_{\mathrm{MVP}}$, the active risk of the shortfall minimizing frontier portfolio is

$$\sigma_s^2 \;=\; \sigma_B^2 - \frac{1}{c} - \frac{1}{d}\left(\mu_B - \frac{b}{c}\right)^2 + \frac{1}{d}\left(\mu_B - \frac{a-b\tau}{b-c\tau}\right)^2 . \qquad (4A.1)$$

Proof. Jorion (2003, pp. 80f.) derives a relationship between expected return and tracking error variance of frontier portfolios. For a frontier portfolio P with $\mu_P \geq \mu_B$, it reads:

$$\mu_P \;=\; \mu_B + \sqrt{d\sigma_s^2 - d\left(\sigma_B^2 - \frac{1}{c}\right) + \left(\mu_B - \frac{b}{c}\right)^2} . \qquad (4A.2)$$

According to proposition 4.7, the set of dominating portfolios is the set of convex combinations of portfolio B^* and $\widehat{B}$. For $\mu_{B^*} = \mu_B$, equation (4A.2) has solution

$$\sigma_s^2 \;=\; \sigma_B^2 - \frac{1}{c} - \frac{1}{d}\left(\mu_B - \frac{b}{c}\right)^2 = \sigma_B^2 - \sigma_{\mathrm{MVP}}^2 - \frac{1}{d}\left(\mu_B - \mu_{\mathrm{MVP}}\right)^2 .$$

This lower bound is due to Jorion (2003, p. 80).

For $\mu_{\widehat{B}} = \frac{b}{c} + \sqrt{(a - b^2/c)\,(\sigma_B^2 - 1/c)}$, the solution is

$$\begin{aligned}
\sigma_s^2 \;&=\; \frac{1}{d}\left(\mu_B - \frac{b}{c} - \sqrt{\left(a - \frac{b^2}{c}\right)\left(\sigma_B^2 - \frac{1}{c}\right)}\right)^2 + \left(\sigma_B^2 - \frac{1}{c}\right) - \frac{1}{d}\left(\mu_B - \frac{b}{c}\right)^2 \\
&=\; 2\left(\sigma_B^2 - \frac{1}{c}\right) - \frac{2}{\sqrt{a - b^2/c}}\sqrt{\sigma_B^2 - 1/c}\left(\mu_B - \frac{b}{c}\right) \\
&=\; 2\left(\sigma_B^2 - \sigma_{\mathrm{MVP}}^2\right) - \frac{2}{\sqrt{d}}\sqrt{\sigma_B^2 - \sigma_{\mathrm{MVP}}^2}\;\left(\mu_B - \mu_{\mathrm{MVP}}\right) .
\end{aligned}$$

With expected return $\mu_P = (a - b\tau)/(b - c\tau)$ of the shortfall minimizing portfolio in proposition 2.6, equation (4A.2) yields equation (4A.1). □

Chapter 5

Delegated Investing and Value at Risk Optimization

Value at Risk (VaR) has established as a standard risk measure for the risk management of investment portfolios. While the portfolio optimization based on VaR as discussed in section 2.4 is well known, the VaR minimization for benchmark-relative portfolio mandates needs further investigation. This chapter describes the VaR optimization of portfolios that are constructed to outperform a benchmark portfolio given a limit on active risk. It is relevant for the risk management of financial institutions that give incentives to portfolio managers to outperform a benchmark. While it is unquestionable that portfolio managers have to take risks to generate superior returns, the more controversial question is "How much risk is optimal?". This chapter is supposed to answer this question.

A standard element of portfolio managers' remuneration is that the compensation depends on the portfolio performance relative to benchmark performance. It induces incentives to portfolio managers to reallocate portfolio weights from a benchmark portfolio and to increase active risk. Risk management controls the managers' risk taking by restricting active risk. While portfolio managers care about staying within active risk limits, risk management is concerned about the level of the portfolio's VaR at the overall level. So, the risk measures that are relevant to active managers and risk management may differ. The chapter presents a principal-agent model for studying such a relationship.

The following sections show how to minimize VaR when portfolio selection is delegated to a tracking error restricted portfolio manager. Active risk limits can be used to control portfolio selection and influence the resulting VaR. Section 5.1 derives the optimal amount of active risk that yields a benchmark relative portfolio with minimum VaR. Section 5.2 derives the optimal active risk for beta restricted portfolios. Section 5.3 shows how active risk and portfolio beta should be chosen to obtain a mean-variance efficient portfolio with minimum VaR. In contrast to the previous chapter, we refrain from discussing the information issues in this chapter.

5.1 Minimizing the VaR for TEV Portfolios

This section studies the optimal control of the delegated portfolio selection with active risk limits when the principal aims at minimizing the portfolio's VaR. The principal hires an agent who aims at outperforming a given benchmark portfolio and restricts benchmark deviations with a tracking error constraint, as illustrated in figure 5.1.

As in the previous chapter, the assumptions 2.1 (frictionless markets), 2.2 (asset returns), 2.4 (normally distributed asset returns) apply. Now, for a given shortfall probability $p = P(R_P < \tau)$, the principal wishes to minimize VaR or, equivalently, maximize the threshold return τ according to assumption 2.3" (Kataoka criterion). She delegates portfolio selection and

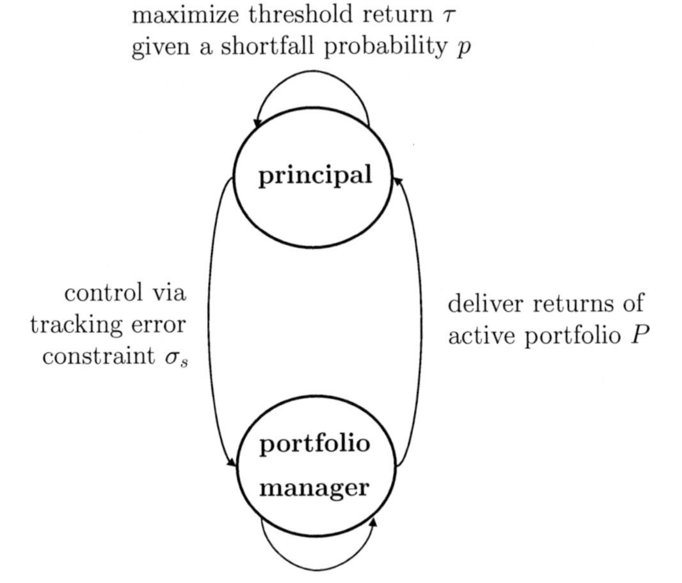

Figure 5.1: Controlling the VaR of a Benchmark-Relative Portfolio via the Tracking Error Constraint

controls the benchmark-relative portfolio selection via constraints. Following assumption 3.1', the agent maximizes expected excess return under the specified constraints.

Problem 5.1 (Minimize the VaR for TEV Portfolios).
Determine the optimal constraint on tracking error such that the VaR of the TEV portfolio is minimized or, equivalently, such that the threshold return is maximized:

$$
\begin{aligned}
\textit{objective:} \quad & \max_{\sigma_s} \tau \\
\textit{constraint:} \quad & P(R_P < \tau) = p \\
& P \textit{ is solution of the TEV problem 3.1(2) with constraint } \sigma_s^2 .
\end{aligned}
$$

Figure 5.2 illustrates the maximum achievable threshold and TEV portfolio for a shortfall probability $p = P(R_B < 0)$ of nominal maintenance of the benchmark. In comparison with a passive investment in the benchmark B, the investor can achieve a higher threshold return with equal shortfall probability by delegating portfolio selection. Given a shortfall probability p and normally distributed asset returns, the shortfall line $\mu_P = \tau + m_p \sigma_P$ has slope $m_p \equiv (\mu_P - \tau)/\sigma_P = \Phi^{-1}(1 - p)$. A necessary condition for the existence of a solution of problem 5.1 is that the slope of the shortfall line is greater than the slope $\sqrt{d}$ of the TEV line's asymptote. Otherwise, there would always exist an intersection of shortfall line and TEV line when the target return is increased. A positive benchmark excess return is guaranteed when the tangent on the TEV line at the benchmark has a slope that is greater than the slope of the shortfall line. By equation (3.5), an upper bound on the slope of the shortfall line is given by $m_p \leq \frac{d\sigma_B}{\mu_B - \mu_{\mathrm{MVP}}}$. The restriction $\sqrt{d} < m_p \leq \frac{d\sigma_B}{\mu_B - \mu_{\mathrm{MVP}}}$ on the slope is equivalent to the condition $\Phi\left(-\frac{d\sigma_B}{\mu_B - \mu_{\mathrm{MVP}}}\right) \leq p < \Phi\left(-\sqrt{d}\right)$ on the shortfall probability.

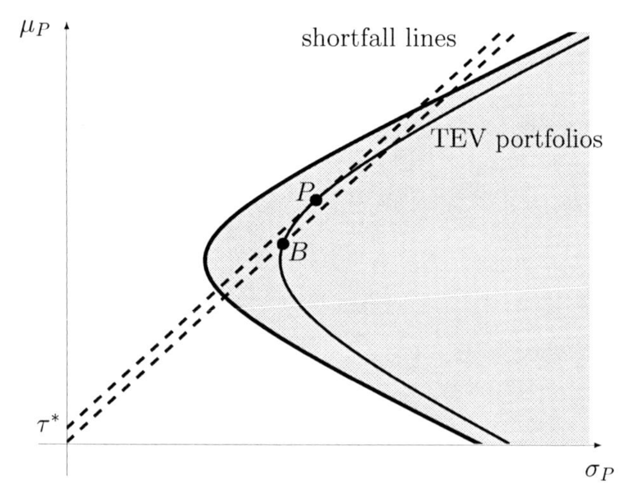

Figure 5.2: Maximum Threshold for TEV Portfolios for a Given Shortfall Probability

Proposition 5.2.
Let $\mu_B > \mu_{\text{MVP}}$ *and* $\Phi\left(-\frac{d\sigma_B}{\mu_B - \mu_{\text{MVP}}}\right) \leq p < \Phi\left(-\sqrt{d}\right)$ *hold. The TEV portfolio with minimum VaR is achieved with tracking error*

$$\sigma_s = \sqrt{\frac{d\sigma_B^2 - (\mu_B - \mu_{\text{MVP}})^2}{m_p^2 - d}} - \frac{1}{\sqrt{d}}(\mu_B - \mu_{\text{MVP}})$$

and the maximum threshold is

$$\tau^* = \mu_{\text{MVP}} - \sqrt{(m_p^2/d - 1)(d\sigma_B^2 - (\mu_B - \mu_{\text{MVP}})^2)}\,.$$

Proof. The threshold return of the shortfall line through a TEV portfolio can be stated as a function of the portfolio's tracking error

$$\tau = \mu_P - m_p\sigma_P = \mu_B + \sqrt{d}\sigma_s - m_p\left(\sigma_B^2 + \frac{2}{\sqrt{d}}\left(\mu_B - \frac{b}{c}\right)\sigma_s + \sigma_s^2\right)^{1/2},$$

where expected return μ_P and standard deviation σ_P of the TEV portfolio are replaced using equations (3.2) and (3.3). The optimal tracking error constraint σ_s results from the conditions $\partial\tau/\partial\sigma_s = 0$ and $\partial^2\tau/\partial\sigma_s^2 < 0$. □

5.2 Minimizing the VaR for TEVBR Portfolios with Given Beta

This section derives the optimal tracking error budget such that the benchmark-relative portfolio selection with fixed standard beta constraint minimizes the portfolio's VaR. As in the previous section, the principal's only control variable is the tracking error constraint. Figure 5.3 illustrates the optimal solution.

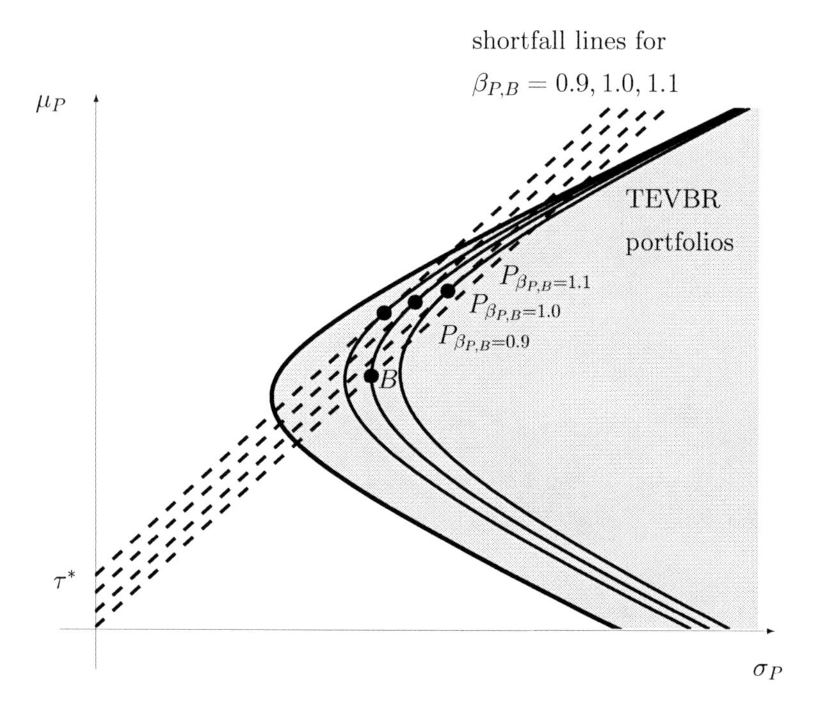

Figure 5.3: Maximum Threshold Return for Fixed Beta and Shortfall Probability with TEVBR Portfolios for $\beta_{P,B} = 0.9, 1.0, 1.1$

Problem 5.3 (Minimize the VaR of TEVBR Portfolios with Given Beta). *Given a fixed beta constraint, determine the optimal constraint on tracking error in the TEVBR problem 3.3(2) such that the threshold return is maximized:*

objective:	$\max_{\sigma_s} \tau$
constraint:	$P(R_P < \tau) = p$
	P is a solution of the TEVBR problem 3.3(2)
	with constraints σ_s^2 *and standard* $\beta_{P,B}$.

Proposition 5.4.
The optimal constraint on tracking error in problem 5.3 is

$$\sigma_s = \frac{\sqrt{\det \boldsymbol{H}\ \sigma^2_{\mathrm{MVP}}(2\beta_{P,B}-1)+(\beta_{P,B}-1)^2 m_p^2\sigma_B^2}}{\sqrt{m_p^2(\sigma_B^2-\sigma^2_{\mathrm{MVP}})-\det \boldsymbol{H}\ \sigma^2_{\mathrm{MVP}}}}\,\sigma_B\,. \tag{5.1}$$

The maximum threshold for TEVBR portfolios with fixed beta and shortfall probability p is

$$\tau = \frac{1}{\sigma_B^2-\sigma^2_{\mathrm{MVP}}}\Big(\mu_{\mathrm{MVP}}\sigma_B^2-\mu_B\sigma^2_{\mathrm{MVP}}+(\mu_B-\mu_{\mathrm{MVP}})\beta_{P,B}\sigma_B^2 \\ -\sqrt{(\sigma^2_{\mathrm{MVP}}+\beta_{P,B}(\beta_{P,B}\sigma_B^2-2\sigma^2_{\mathrm{MVP}}))(m_p^2(\sigma_B^2-\sigma^2_{\mathrm{MVP}})-\det\boldsymbol{H}\sigma^2_{\mathrm{MVP}})}\,\sigma_B\Big). \tag{5.2}$$

Proof. The equation of the threshold shortfall line through a TEVBR portfolio reads $\mu_P = \tau + m_p\sigma_P$. The threshold return $\tau = \mu_P - m_p\sigma_P$ is a function of σ_s after replacing σ_P and $\mu_P = \mu_B + G$ as given in equations (3.10) and (3.11). The optimal tracking error σ_s can be solved for using the conditions $\partial\tau/\partial\sigma_s = 0$ and $\sigma_s > 0$. □

5.3 Minimizing the VaR with Efficient TEVBR Portfolios

If the investor strives for a frontier portfolio with minimum VaR, she can still delegate portfolio selection to a portfolio manager who composes benchmark-relative portfolios. She has to control the delegated portfolio selection with beta and tracking error constraints simultaneously.

Problem 5.5 (Minimize VaR for TEVBR Portfolios Using β and σ_s). *Determine the optimal beta constraint and tracking error constraint in the TEVBR problem 3.3(2) such that the threshold return is maximized:*

$$\begin{array}{ll} \textit{objective:} & \max\limits_{\sigma_s,\beta_{P,B}} \tau \\ \textit{constraint:} & P(R_P < \tau) = p\,. \\ & \textit{P is a solution of the TEVBR problem 3.3(2)} \\ & \textit{with constraints } \sigma_s \textit{ and } \beta_{P,B}\,. \end{array}$$

Without constraints, the frontier portfolio that maximizes the threshold return for shortfall probability p is given in proposition 2.8. This portfolio can also be achieved with a TEVBR portfolio as a solution of problem 5.5. Figure 5.4 illustrates TEVBR portfolios. They are very close to the efficient frontier, since beta is chosen optimally. If the tracking error constraint is also optimal, the portfolio manager constructs a TEVBR portfolio that is mean-variance efficient.

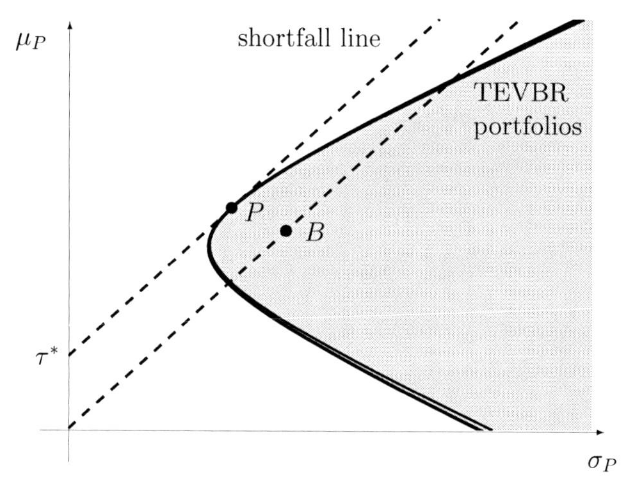

Figure 5.4: Maximum Threshold and Mean-Variance Efficient TEVBR Portfolio P for Given Shortfall Probability

Proposition 5.6.
Given a fixed threshold shortfall probability p, $p < \Phi(-\sqrt{d})$, the maximum threshold return of problem 5.5 is given by equation (2.20). It is achieved with the solution of the TEVBR problem 3.3(2) with beta factor constraint

$$\beta_{P,B} = \frac{\sigma^2_{\mathrm{MVP}}}{\sigma^2_B} + \frac{(\mu_B - \mu_{\mathrm{MVP}})\sqrt{\sigma^2_B - \sigma^2_{\mathrm{MVP}}}\,\sigma_{\mathrm{MVP}}}{\sqrt{m_p^2\sigma_B^2 - (\det \boldsymbol{H} + m_p^2)\sigma^2_{\mathrm{MVP}} - (\mu_B - \mu_{\mathrm{MVP}})^2}\ \sigma^2_B}$$

and tracking error constraint given in equation (5.1). The optimal TEVBR portfolio for the maximum threshold of problem 5.5 is identical to the frontier portfolio given in proposition 2.8.

Proof. The frontier portfolio of proposition 2.8 satisfies the shortfall probability condition for the maximum threshold. Its beta can be derived from the first order condition $\partial\tau/\partial\beta_{P,B} = 0$, where τ is given in equation (5.2). □

Chapter 6

An Asset Pricing Model with Delegating and Shortfall Probability Minimizing Investors

In financial decision making, some threshold returns are more relevant than others. For example nominal or real maintenance of capital can be aimed for with a threshold return of zero or inflation rate, respectively. Minimum target returns are guaranteed by many policies of pension funds. These returns are also often thresholds for managers' performance evaluation besides of evaluation relative to a benchmark. Managers might anticipate that they lose clients or their job if their portfolio return falls short a threshold. If there are many market participants that minimize shortfall probability according to one threshold return, such behavior can influence market equilibrium and have implications for asset pricing. Chapter 4 shows how investors can maximize the Sharpe ratio or implement a safety first approach when delegating investment decisions. This chapter explores the implications on asset pricing in the case that a substantial part of investors pursues such a strategy.

This chapter extends the Capital Asset Pricing Model (CAPM) for delegated investing in the presence of a common threshold return. Section 6.1 recalls basic assumptions and results of the CAPM. Section 6.2 elaborates the differences in assumptions that are necessary to account for delegated investing and explores the risk-return relationship in market equilibrium.

6.1 The Capital Asset Pricing Model

Section 2.5 shows how a single investor invests optimally in efficient portfolios when a riskless asset is available. This section recalls implications on asset pricing given that all market participants invest in such efficient portfolios. This Capital Asset Pricing Model was pioneered by Sharpe (1964), Lintner (1965), and Mossin (1966). The main result is the security market line, equation (6.1), which states that the expected excess return of a single asset is linear in market risk. A similar relationship also holds in case of absence of a riskless asset, as is shown by Black (1972).

The CAPM is based on the assumption 2.1 (frictionless market), assumption 2.3 (mean-variance criterion), and the following assumption of homogeneously informed investors.

Assumption 6.1 (Homogeneous Information).
Market participants have identical estimates of the assets' expected returns, variance, and covariances.

If a riskless asset is traded and all investors spend their wealth in efficient portfolios only, all individual proportions of wealth spent in risky assets are identical and given by the tangency portfolio as shown in section 2.5. The *market portfolio* is the portfolio of all wealth spent in risky assets. The relative compositions of market portfolio and tangency portfolio coincide as a result of wealth spent efficiently in identical risky proportions:

$$\mathbf{x}_M = \mathbf{x}_T \ .$$

In market equilibrium, all market participants invest in the riskless asset and the market portfolio. This implies that the market return is the only risk factor for all portfolio returns. The relationship of expected return and volatility of *efficient portfolios* is called capital market line and is given by equation (2.24). As a result of this market equilibrium, the expected excess return of a *single asset* depends linearly on the asset's sensitivity $\beta_{i,M} \equiv \mathrm{Cov}(R_i, R_M)/\mathrm{Var}(R_M)$ to market returns.

Proposition 6.1 (Security Market Line).
Let assumptions 2.1 (frictionless market), 2.3 (mean-variance criterion), 6.1 (homogeneous information) as well as assumption 2.2 (risky assets) or 2.2' (riskless and risky assets) hold. Then, the relationship of an asset's expected excess return and beta is linear in market equilibrium.

a) *If a riskless asset is available by assumption 2.2', the market portfolio is efficient and the security market line reads*

$$\begin{aligned} \mu_i(\beta_{i,M}) &= r_f + (\mu_M - r_f)\,\beta_{i,M} \\ &= r_f + \frac{a - 2br_f + cr_f^2}{b - cr_f}\beta_{i,M} \ . \end{aligned} \tag{6.1}$$

b) *If a riskless asset is not available by assumption 2.2 and the market portfolio is efficient, the security market line reads*

$$\begin{aligned} \mu_i(\beta_{i,M}) &= \frac{a - b\mu_M}{b - c\mu_M} + \left(\mu_M - \frac{a - b\mu_M}{b - c\mu_M}\right)\beta_{i,M} \\ &= \frac{a - b\mu_M}{b - c\mu_M} + \frac{-a + 2b\mu_M - c\mu_M^2}{-b + c\mu_M}\beta_{i,M} \ . \end{aligned} \tag{6.2}$$

Proof. a) Under the given assumptions, section 2.5 shows that market participants invest their wealth in an efficient tangency portfolio T corresponding to the riskless investment if available. Given expected return $\mu_T = \frac{a-br_f}{b-cr_f}$, the variance of return is $\sigma_T^2 = \frac{a-2b\mu_T+c\mu_T^2}{ac-b^2}$ according to equation (2.2).

The vector of covariances of all assets with the tangency portfolio can be written using equation (2.1) as

$$\boldsymbol{V}\mathbf{x}_T = (\boldsymbol{\mu}\ \mathbf{1})\,\boldsymbol{A}^{-1}\begin{pmatrix}\mu_T\\ 1\end{pmatrix}$$

as well as

$$\boldsymbol{V}\mathbf{x}_T = \frac{\boldsymbol{V}\mathbf{x}_T}{\mathbf{x}_T'\boldsymbol{V}\mathbf{x}_T}\mathbf{x}_T'\boldsymbol{V}\mathbf{x}_T = \boldsymbol{\beta}_{|T}\frac{a-2b\mu_T+c\mu_T^2}{ac-b^2},$$

where $\boldsymbol{\beta}_{|T} = (\beta_{1,T},\ldots,\beta_{n,T})'$ denotes the vector of betas

$$\beta_{i,T} \equiv \frac{\mathrm{Cov}(R_i, R_T)}{\mathrm{Var}(R_T)}, \quad i = 1,\ldots,n$$

of the assets. Since both vectors of covariances are equal, equating both expressions and solving for the expected return of the assets yields

$$\boldsymbol{\mu} = \frac{a-b\mu_T}{b-c\mu_T}\mathbf{1} + \frac{-a+2b\mu_T-c\mu_T^2}{-b+c\mu_T}\boldsymbol{\beta}_{|T}\,. \tag{6.3}$$

Since all market participants invest in the tangency portfolio and the riskless investment exclusively, the tangency portfolio and market portfolio coincide and $\mu_M = \mu_T$ holds. If a riskless investment is available, replacing the expected return μ_T with $(a-br_f)/(b-cr_f)$ and taking the ith entry yields equation (6.1).

b) If no riskless investment is available, above derivation also holds when the tangency portfolio is replaced with the efficient market portfolio. The ith entry of equation (6.3) and $\mu_T = \mu_M$ yield equation (6.2). □

6.2 A Delegated-Agent Asset-Pricing Model

A first attempt to study the implications of delegated investing on asset pricing is made by Brennan (1993). He suggests an economy with mean-variance optimizing investors and institutional investors who select portfolios relative to a benchmark portfolio. The resulting market portfolio is a combination of a mean-variance efficient portfolio and benchmark-relative TEV portfolio. In market equilibrium, expected returns are characterized by a two-factor model with factors benchmark and market portfolio. Assets with higher covariance with the benchmark have, ceteris paribus, a lower expected return. Brennan's empirical evidence fails to support the model's predictions, but Gómez and Zapatero (2003) find empirical evidence for Brennan's two-factor model.

Cornell and Roll (2005) also stress the importance of institutional investors in asset pricing and suggest to extend the CAPM to account for delegated investing. They assume the active manager's compensation schedule to be a trade off between excess return and tracking error volatility. They find that "when all investment decisions are delegated, the preferences and beliefs of individuals would be completely superseded by the objective functions of managers". In their model, the asset prices in market equilibrium result from the trade off between excess return and tracking error in the managers' compensation plan. However, they do not account for the interaction of principal and agent when negotiating the contract. The model presented below advances Cornell and Roll's delegated-agent asset-pricing model by accounting for the principal's objectives. Our approach emphasizes the investors' perspective and their objective to minimize the shortfall probability or to maximize the Sharpe ratio. The principal is able to control the agent's portfolio selection via active risk budgeting. However, the manager's objective is still relevant, since the principal's wealth is invested in benchmark-relative portfolios. As a result, asset pricing depends on the benchmark portfolio as well as market relevant threshold returns. Furthermore, while in their approach only TEV portfolios are active managed portfolios, we also include TEVBR portfolios in our analysis.

Asset pricing has also been studied in the case that the investors' portfolio choice is determined with downside risk measures such as shortfall probability, expected shortfall, or shortfall variance. Hogan and Warren (1974) and Bawa and Lindenberg (1977) derive CAPM-like models based on downside risk measures with the risk-free rate as benchmark return. Harlow and Rao (1989) generalize these models and derive equilibrium models based on mean-lower partial moments for an arbitrary target rate of return. Recently, Ang, Chen, and Xing (2006) test an equilibrium model with downside risk and find empirical evidence for a premium for stocks with high downside risk. The following model brings the aspect of delegated investing to shortfall probability minimizing asset pricing models.

In our model, there are two types of portfolio managers who trade on a market based on assumptions 2.1 (frictionless market) and 2.2 (risky assets): The passive managers invest everything in a benchmark portfolio B. The active managers select portfolios relative to the benchmark portfolio B, and they have homogeneous estimates of the expected asset returns $\boldsymbol{\mu}$ and their covariances $\boldsymbol{V}$. A fraction w of total wealth is invested with the active managers, the rest $1-w$ with the passive managers. These assumptions underlie also the model framework of Cornell and Roll (2005). We extend their assumptions with assumptions concerning the investors' tastes and information asymmetry. For our model, we assume that there is a fixed threshold return τ that is market wide accepted as an important threshold. The delegating investors' objective is either a) to maximize the Sharpe ratio (then $\tau = r_f$) or b) to minimize the threshold shortfall probability $P(R_P < \tau)$ by Roy's criterion 2.3' when asset returns are normally distributed by assumption 2.4. The investors control the agents' portfolio selection via active risk budgeting as discussed in sections 4.4, 4.5, and 4.6.

They may choose risk constraints as given by assumption 4.2 (principal's control variables) while active managers maximize benchmark excess return given these restrictions as indicated by assumption 3.1' (maximize excess return). Investors have partial or total information as given by assumption 4.1(b), (c), and (d) (information asymmetry).[1] The assumption 6.1 is restricted to homogeneous information within the group of active managers and within the group of investors.

Proposition 6.2.
Given above assumptions, the relationship between an asset's expected return and its beta in market equilibrium depends on the level of the investors' information about the financial market.

a) *Given information level* $\{\mu_B, \sigma_B, \mu_{\text{MVP}}, d\}$, *it is*

$$\mu_j = \mu_{\text{MVP}} + (\mu_M - \mu_{\text{MVP}})\,\beta_{j,M} + K\,(\beta_{j,M}\beta_{M,B} - \beta_{j,B}) \ , \quad (6.4)$$

where K *is a positive constant and defined as*

$$K \equiv \frac{\sqrt{d\sigma_B^2}}{w\sigma_s} = \frac{d\sigma_B^2(\mu_{\text{MVP}} - \tau)}{w(d\sigma_B^2 - (\mu_B - \tau)(\mu_B - \mu_{\text{MVP}}))} \ .$$

b) *Given information level* $\{\mu_B, \sigma_B, \boldsymbol{A}\}$, *it is*

$$\mu_j = \tau + (\mu_M - \tau)\beta_{j,M} + K\,(\beta_{j,M}\beta_{M,B} - \beta_{j,B}) \ , \quad (6.5)$$

where $K \equiv (\mu_{\text{MVP}} - \tau)\frac{\sigma_B^2}{\sigma_{\text{MVP}}^2}\frac{1-w}{w}$.

c) *Given information level* $\{\boldsymbol{\mu}, \boldsymbol{V}\}$, *there is no need to delegate and the principals invest in the tangency portfolio with* $\mu_M = \mu_T = \frac{a-b\tau}{b-c\tau}$. *The returns are described by the security market line (6.2) of the Black-CAPM.*

[1] Fully informed investors are also considered in Brennan (1993, p. 11 et seq.). Brennan concludes that the CAPM-version of Black holds in this case.

Proof. Since there are only two representative managers and there is only one market relevant threshold return in the economy, the market equilibrium is rather simple. The market portfolio consists of the active managed portfolio $\mathbf{x}_A = \mathbf{x}_B + \boldsymbol{s}$ as well as of the passive portfolio $\mathbf{x}_B$, weighted with the proportions w and $1 - w$, respectively:

$$\mathbf{x}_M = w\mathbf{x}_A + (1-w)\mathbf{x}_B = w(\mathbf{x}_B + \boldsymbol{s}) + (1-w)\mathbf{x}_B = \mathbf{x}_B + w\boldsymbol{s} \ .$$

Investors choose type and value of portfolio constraints depending on their information level. Accordingly, the active portfolio is a shortfall minimizing TEV or TEVBR portfolio as discussed in section 4.7. For each information level, we first calculate the vector of covariance between market and single asset returns, then the variance of market return. After rewriting the covariance vector, the relation between an asset's return and its beta is derived.

a) If investors know $\{\mu_B, \sigma_B, \mu_{\mathrm{MVP}}, d\}$, they can specify an optimal tracking error constraint as given in proposition 4.2 such that the manager composes a TEV with least threshold shortfall probability among all TEV portfolios. With $\boldsymbol{s}$ given in equation (3.1) and σ_s from equation (4.1), the vector of covariances between returns of the market portfolio and single assets reads

$$\begin{aligned} \boldsymbol{V}\mathbf{x}_M &= \boldsymbol{V}\mathbf{x}_B + w\boldsymbol{V}\boldsymbol{s} = \boldsymbol{V}\mathbf{x}_B + \frac{w\sigma_s}{\sqrt{d}}\left(\boldsymbol{\mu} - \frac{b}{c}\mathbf{1}\right) \\ &= \boldsymbol{\beta}_{|B}\sigma_B^2 + \frac{w\sigma_s}{\sqrt{d}}\left(\boldsymbol{\mu} - \frac{b}{c}\mathbf{1}\right) , \end{aligned} \tag{6.6}$$

where $\boldsymbol{\beta}_{|P} = (\beta_{1,P}, \ldots, \beta_{n,P})'$ denotes the vector of individual asset betas on a portfolio P. With variance of market return

$$\mathbf{x}_M\boldsymbol{V}\mathbf{x}_M = \mathbf{x}_M\boldsymbol{V}\mathbf{x}_B + \frac{w\sigma_s}{\sqrt{d}}\left(\mu_M - \frac{b}{c}\right) ,$$

the covariance vector can also be written as

$$\begin{aligned} \boldsymbol{V}\mathbf{x}_M &= \frac{\boldsymbol{V}\mathbf{x}_M}{\mathbf{x}_M'\boldsymbol{V}\mathbf{x}_M}\mathbf{x}_M'\boldsymbol{V}\mathbf{x}_M = \boldsymbol{\beta}_{|M}\mathbf{x}_M'\boldsymbol{V}\mathbf{x}_M \\ &= \boldsymbol{\beta}_{|M}\left(\mathbf{x}_M\boldsymbol{V}\mathbf{x}_B + \frac{w\sigma_s}{\sqrt{d}}\left(\mu_M - \frac{b}{c}\right)\right) \\ &= \boldsymbol{\beta}_{|M}\beta_{M,B}\sigma_B^2 + \boldsymbol{\beta}_{|M}\frac{w\sigma_s}{\sqrt{d}}\left(\mu_M - \frac{b}{c}\right) . \end{aligned} \tag{6.7}$$

Since the covariance vectors in equations (6.6) and (6.7) are equal, the vector equation of the cross-sectional relationship between betas and expected returns can be derived:

$$\boldsymbol{\mu} = \frac{b}{c}\mathbf{1} + \boldsymbol{\beta}_{|M}\left(\mu_M - \frac{b}{c}\right) + \frac{\sqrt{d}\sigma_B^2}{w\sigma_s}\left(\boldsymbol{\beta}_{|M}\beta_{M,B} - \boldsymbol{\beta}_{|B}\right) .$$

Using $\mu_{\text{MVP}} = \frac{b}{c}$, the jth entry in this system of equations is

$$\begin{aligned} \mu_j &= \mu_{\text{MVP}} + \beta_{j,M}\left(\mu_M - \mu_{\text{MVP}}\right) + \frac{\sqrt{d}\sigma_B^2}{w\sigma_s}\left(\beta_{j,M}\beta_{M,B} - \beta_{j,B}\right) \\ &= \mu_{\text{MVP}} + \beta_{j,M}\left(\mu_M - \mu_{\text{MVP}}\right) + K\left(\beta_{j,M}\beta_{M,B} - \beta_{j,B}\right) , \end{aligned}$$

where, using equation (4.1), the constant K is defined by

$$K \equiv \frac{\sqrt{d}\sigma_B^2}{w\sigma_s} = \frac{d\sigma_B^2(\mu_{\text{MVP}} - \tau)}{w(d\sigma_B^2 - (\mu_B - \tau)(\mu_B - \mu_{\text{MVP}}))} .$$

b) Given information level $\{\mu_B, \sigma_B, \boldsymbol{A}\}$, investors choose to delegate investments to portfolio managers that compose TEVBR portfolios with excess return $G = \overline{G}$ and portfolio constraint $\beta_{P,B}$ of proposition 4.6. With these constraints and $\boldsymbol{s}$ as given in equation (3.8), the vector of covariances between market return and single assets is

$$\begin{aligned} \boldsymbol{V}\mathbf{x}_M &= \boldsymbol{V}\mathbf{x}_B + w\boldsymbol{V}\boldsymbol{s} \\ &= \boldsymbol{V}\mathbf{x}_B + w\left(\boldsymbol{V}\mathbf{x}_B \;\; \boldsymbol{\mu} \;\; \mathbf{1}\right)\boldsymbol{H}^{-1}\begin{pmatrix} (\beta_{P,B} - 1)\sigma_B^2 \\ G \\ 0 \end{pmatrix} . \end{aligned} \tag{6.8}$$

With variance of market return

$$\mathbf{x}_M' \boldsymbol{V} \mathbf{x}_M = \mathbf{x}_M' \boldsymbol{V} \mathbf{x}_B + w \left(\mathbf{x}_M' \boldsymbol{V} \mathbf{x}_B \quad \mu_M \quad 1 \right) \boldsymbol{H}^{-1} \begin{pmatrix} (\beta_{P,B} - 1)\sigma_B^2 \\ G \\ 0 \end{pmatrix},$$

the covariance vector can also be written as

$$\begin{aligned} \boldsymbol{V} \mathbf{x}_M &= \frac{\boldsymbol{V} \mathbf{x}_M}{\mathbf{x}_M' \boldsymbol{V} \mathbf{x}_M} \mathbf{x}_M' \boldsymbol{V} \mathbf{x}_M = \boldsymbol{\beta}_{|M} \mathbf{x}_M' \boldsymbol{V} \mathbf{x}_M \\ &= \boldsymbol{\beta}_{|M} \mathbf{x}_M' \boldsymbol{V} \mathbf{x}_B \\ &\quad + \boldsymbol{\beta}_{|M} w \left(\mathbf{x}_M' \boldsymbol{V} \mathbf{x}_B \quad \mu_M \quad 1 \right) \boldsymbol{H}^{-1} \begin{pmatrix} (\beta_{P,B} - 1)\sigma_B^2) \\ G \\ 0 \end{pmatrix}. \end{aligned} \tag{6.9}$$

Since the covariance vectors in equations (6.8) and (6.9) are equal, the vector of expected returns of the single assets can be solved for:

$$\begin{aligned} \boldsymbol{\mu} &= \mu_M \boldsymbol{\beta}_{|M} + \frac{(-a + b\mu_B)(\beta_{P,B} - 1)\sigma_B^2 + (\mu_B - b\sigma_B^2)G}{(b - c\mu_B)(\beta_{P,B} - 1)\sigma_B^2 + (\mu_B - b\sigma_B^2)G} (-\mathbf{1} + \boldsymbol{\beta}_{|M}) \\ &\quad + \frac{\frac{\det \boldsymbol{H}}{w} + (ac - b^2)(\beta_{P,B} - 1)\sigma_B^2 + (b - c\mu_B)G}{(b - c\mu_B)(\beta_{P,B} - 1)\sigma_B^2 + (-1 + c\sigma_B^2)G} \sigma_B^2 \left(\boldsymbol{\beta}_{|M} \beta_{M,B} - \boldsymbol{\beta}_{|B} \right). \end{aligned}$$

With excess return $G = \overline{G}$ and portfolio constraint $\beta_{P,B}$ of proposition 4.6, we get after simplifying

$$\boldsymbol{\mu} = \tau \mathbf{1} + (\mu_M - \tau) \boldsymbol{\beta}_{|M} + K \left(\boldsymbol{\beta}_{|M} \beta_{M,B} - \boldsymbol{\beta}_{|B} \right),$$

where $K = (\frac{b}{c} - \tau) c \sigma_B^2 \frac{1-w}{w} = (\mu_{\text{MVP}} - \tau) \frac{\sigma_B^2}{\sigma_{\text{MVP}}^2} \frac{1-w}{w}$.

c) Without information asymmetry and market frictions, there is no need for investors to delegate and the standard risk-return relationship of the Black-CAPM results. □

Chapter 7

Decentralizing Portfolio Selection

Strategic asset allocation and active risk allocation are usually studied and implemented separately. Following this standard approach to set up an active managed portfolio, chapter 2 presents asset allocation and section 7.2 below presents active risk allocation when both tasks are implemented independently of each other. A basic prerequisite is that total active risk is specified exogenously. However, separate optimal solutions for asset and active risk allocation may yield suboptimal solutions for the combined allocation problem. This chapter contributes to the literature by merging both allocation problems and solving them simultaneously. The key to the optimal solution of most of the portfolio selection problems considered is the optimal total active risk that is derived endogenously. After the optimal total active risk is calculated, the asset and active risk allocations depend on total active risk and can be done separately.

The models presented in this chapter differ in several aspects from the models of previous chapters. First, by extending from one to several strategies to generate excess return, we allow for the combination and diversification across several active strategies. Second, while the benchmark portfolio was given in previous chapters, now the strategic allocation as well as the active risk allocation are optimized simultaneously. Third, the passive mean-variance frontier is extended by active strategies.

Section 7.1 discusses practical issues of investment companies that decentralize investment decisions and outsource parts of their fund management and fund administration. Active risk allocation problems are reviewed in section 7.2. Section 7.3 derives the optimal active risk allocation given an additional shortfall constraint on the active return. The main contribution of this chapter is the simultaneous asset and active risk allocation in section 7.4. The simultaneous allocation is also solved for the safety first approach and for minimizing the VaR in sections 7.5 and 7.6, respectively.

7.1 Overlay Portfolio Management

While the strategic as well as the tactical asset allocation are typically decided upon by one entity, as discussed in section 4.2, active strategies are implemented simultaneously by a set of portfolio managers. The trading activities of separately managed portfolios need to be coordinated and customized to the client's investment policy. Instead of implementing the client's investment policy in each of the managed accounts, overlay portfolio management focuses on implementing customized investment solutions across portfolios.

German investment companies ("Kapitalanlagegesellschaften", KAGs) are permitted to outsource investment advisory responsibilities to third parties since July 1, 2002.[1] Master KAGs provide services that help corporate investors with the outsourcing of fund management and administration

[1]See the amendment of the Act on Investment Companies ("Gesetz zur weiteren Fortentwicklung des Finanzplatzes Deutschland, Viertes Finanzmarktförderungsgesetz", Artikel 3 "Änderung des Gesetzes über Kapitalanlagegesellschaften, KAGG"), effective on July 1, 2002. The KAGG act merged into the act "Investmentgesetz", effective on January 1, 2004.

services. Besides investment companies, outsourcing fund management is also relevant for investors who do not regard asset management as a core competency such as e.g. managers of corporate pension funds. Investors can delegate the consolidation of their separately managed portfolios to Master KAGs and benefit from uniform account reports which enables the investor to better compare their performance. Clients might benefit from better quality of portfolio management, since a Master KAG revises the management of sub-funds regularly. The following fund administration and management services are suitable for outsourcing to Master KAGs:

- fund accounting,
- centralized fund administration and consolidated reporting,
- tax and transaction cost analysis and customization,
- performance and risk attribution and fund controlling.

Master KAGs can offer these services under increasing economies of scale. Increased demands of clients and regulators in the fields of risk management and fund accounting furthers the transfer of administration services such as performing compliance checks and producing regulatory reports. As an intermediary between account managers and depositary bank, Master KAGs may also take over the coordination of the trading activities of separate managed accounts and conduct the advised transactions. This adds the benefits of a direct ownership of security positions: First, it enables to address client specific tax issues at the investor level and avoid possible tax inefficiencies of separately managed accounts as well as of mutual funds that cannot be customized to the client's tax issues.[2] Second, trading costs can be reduced when rebalancing the portfolio by consolidating the managers' investment decisions and coordinating client-directed contributions and withdrawals.

[2]See e.g. the article by Stein and McIntire (2003) that focuses specifically on tax benefits.

Another major benefit of consolidating separate accounts is that risk management can be centralized and that the client's risk policy can be addressed at the overall portfolio level. The risk management of the overall risk exposure is referred to as risk overlay. A risk overlay mainly contributes to the portfolio performance by efficiently allocating risk resources. At the beginning of an overlay management mandate, the primary objective of the delegated investment process and risk management is established. Typical objectives are to maintain the invested capital at a 95 % or 99 % confidence level, or to outperform an absolute return target or a strategic benchmark, possibly with a certain probability. The overlay manager is assigned the responsibility to maintain risks within a given limit which is measured e.g. by the portfolio's VaR. In this way, the principal delegates the task of overall risk controlling to the risk overlay manager. Within the set risk limit, the overlay manager allocates risk budgets individually to the asset managers and controls the resulting risk proportions after market movements. The risk exposures need to be communicated and adapted continuously to changes in market volatility in order to meet the investor's objective.

Risks of benchmark-relative mandates can be hedged more easily than risks of absolute return mandates. Given an index as benchmark, the risks of the index can be hedged if index futures are available.[3] Trading market risk with futures is a cost-efficient instrument to reduce exposure in market risk without terminating or even having to inform the portfolio managers. This procedure separates two aspects of decentralized investing: alpha production and overlay risk management. Adding a risk overlay allows the investor to delegate the responsibility to generate alpha to asset managers and to delegate the risk management to the overlay manager. Active asset managers can concentrate on outperforming the benchmark while the total portfolio risk is managed on the overlay level. Despite that

[3]When an active managed portfolio is turned market neutral with financial instruments and the net position is self financing, the position is also known as portable alpha source.

the overlay managers may be assigned a VaR limit, the overlay management might control the asset managers via active risk limits, specifically in case of benchmark-relative portfolio selection. So, overlay portfolio management puts decentralized investment decisions under an umbrella of centralized risk management.

The contribution of overlay portfolio management to the overall portfolio's performance differs from that of alpha strategies by its top-down approach. Beside the risk overlay, overlay portfolio management can yield additional earnings with market timing on the overall level. Market timing is the management of the optimal market exposure during times of down- and up-turning markets. It is easer to change the market exposure with futures than with a reallocation of wealth among asset classes. An overlay management of beta risks also aims at explicitly controlling for downside risks in order to secure minimum absolute returns.[4] In total, overlay portfolio management allows to unbundle active managed accounts from beta risks and to secure the client's absolute investment objective.

7.2 Active Risk Allocation

A central element of decentralizing portfolio selection to multiple managers is assigning active risk limits. This section reviews the literature on active risk allocation and recalls the optimal active risk allocation in a basic model framework. Active portfolio management actively deviates from benchmark positions in order to generate excess return. The reallocation of wealth is self-financing and is called active strategy. Assigning active risk limits to active strategies is referred to as active risk budgeting, active risk allocation, or tracking error allocation, since risk

[4]Herold, Maurer, Stamos, and Vo (2007) compare shortfall risk-based strategies of managing dynamically the overall risk exposure.

limits in terms of tracking error are assigned to active managers or their strategies. The expected success of an active strategy can be characterized by its information ratio, the ratio of active return and active risk: $IR \equiv$ expected active return/active risk. It can be derived either from from ex ante expectations or ex post performance data.

Table 7.1 reviews risk allocation models when active strategies are involved. The aim is to maximize the expected excess return, or equivalently, the information ratio of the overall active portfolio given a certain active risk budget. Blitz and Hottinga (2001) investigate the problem of maximizing the portfolio's information ratio given a total active risk budget and uncorrelated active strategies. They show that the optimal allocation of active risk $\sigma^*_{s_i}$ is proportional to the information ratio IR_i. Lee (2000) and Lee and Lam (2001) derive the optimal active risk allocation for the case of correlated active returns. For further reference, the optimal solution for given information ratios instead of given active returns is recalled below in proposition 7.2. The uncertainty of the excess return of a strategy can also be interpreted as uncertainty of the information ratio of the strategy or manager. Molenkamp (2004) proposes to calculate confidence intervals for the information ratio and to constrain the probability of the excess return falling short a threshold return. Section 7.3 derives the outstanding closed form solution of this problem. Scherer (2004, p. 243) investigates the optimal allocation of fund wealth to active managers in the presence of an excess return target. Nevertheless, he also argues that choosing active risk allocation allows greater flexibility than using weight allocation for several reasons. First, possible constraints on physical investments are no longer binding. Second, talented managers might be tied up in small benchmark allocations. Active risk allocation has impact on the amount of active risk only and correctly assigns a large part of the risk budget to the best managers. Manager weight allocation has to consider passive risks additionally and is less flexible in transferring alpha.

Table 7.1: Literature on Active Risk Allocation Models

Author	Optimization problem	Solution
Active risk allocation when active returns are uncorrelated		
Blitz and Hottinga (2001)	$\max_{\boldsymbol{\sigma}_s} \frac{1}{\overline{\sigma}_{s,\text{target}}} \sum_{i=1}^m IR_i \sigma_{s_i}$	$\sigma^*_{s_i} = \frac{IR_i}{IR_P}\overline{\sigma}_{s,\text{target}}$, $i = 1, \ldots, m$,
	$\sum_{i=1}^m \sigma^2_{s_i} = \overline{\sigma}^2_{s,\text{target}}$	where $IR^2_P = \sum_{i=1}^m IR^2_i$
Active risk allocation with correlated active returns		
Lee (2000),	$\max_{\boldsymbol{\sigma}_s} IR_P$	$\boldsymbol{\sigma}^*_s = \frac{\boldsymbol{V}^{-1}_\alpha \boldsymbol{\alpha}}{\sqrt{\boldsymbol{\alpha}'\boldsymbol{V}^{-1}_\alpha \boldsymbol{\alpha}}}\overline{\sigma}_{s,\text{target}}$
Lee and Lam (2001)	$\sum_i \sum_j \sigma_{s_i}\sigma_{s_j}\rho_{s_i,s_j} = \overline{\sigma}^2_{s,\text{target}}$	
Active risk allocation with a shortfall constraint on active return when information ratios are risky		
Molenkamp (2004)	$\max_{\boldsymbol{\sigma}_s} E[\boldsymbol{IR}]'\boldsymbol{\sigma}_s$	no solution provided
	$\boldsymbol{\sigma}'_s \boldsymbol{\Sigma} \boldsymbol{\sigma}_s \leq \overline{\sigma}^2_{s,\text{target}}$	solution is derived in section 7.3
	$P\left(\sum_{i=1}^m IR_i \sigma_{s_i} < \tau\right) \leq p$	
Allocation of fund weight $\mathbf{x} = (x_1, \ldots, x_n)'$ to active portfolio managers		
Scherer (2004, p. 243)	$\min_{\mathbf{x}} \sum_i \sum_j x_i x_j \sigma_{i,j}$	$\mathbf{x}^* = \frac{\boldsymbol{V}^{-1}_s \boldsymbol{\mu}_s}{\boldsymbol{\mu}'_s \boldsymbol{V}^{-1}_s \boldsymbol{\mu}_s}\mu_{s,\text{target}}$
	$\sum_i x_i \mu_{s_i} = \mu_{s,\text{target}}$	

This table provides an overview on active risk allocation models. Vectors and matrices are set in boldface. In the problem studied by Lee (2000) and Lee and Lam (2001), the vector $\boldsymbol{\alpha}$ denotes the expected active returns of strategies with identical tracking error 1%, and $\boldsymbol{V}_\alpha$ is the covariance matrix of active returns. The matrix $\boldsymbol{\Sigma}$ is the correlation matrix of active return strategies. Prespecified upper limits on shortfall probability and total active risk are denoted p and $\overline{\sigma}_{s,\text{target}}$, respectively.

The following analysis is based on the assumption 2.1 (frictionless market) and the following

Assumption 7.1 (Active Strategies).
Let $\boldsymbol{IR} = (IR_1, \ldots, IR_m)'$ *denote the information ratios of* m *investment strategies. These active strategies can be scaled without loss of information ratio. The active returns of the strategies are correlated with positive definite correlation matrix* $\boldsymbol{\Sigma}$*, and they are uncorrelated with the* n *asset returns.*

In the following, we often personify the m strategies with m managers who are able to develop strategies with given information ratios. In contrast to the chapters 3 – 6, we do not derive the active strategies but assume them to be already developed and characterized by their information ratios. Given a risk budget σ_{s_i}, the ith active strategy has expected excess return $IR_i\sigma_{s_i}$. Figure 7.1 illustrates the linear relationship of active risk and active return in case of allocation to single strategies as well as in case of optimal risk allocation to all strategies.

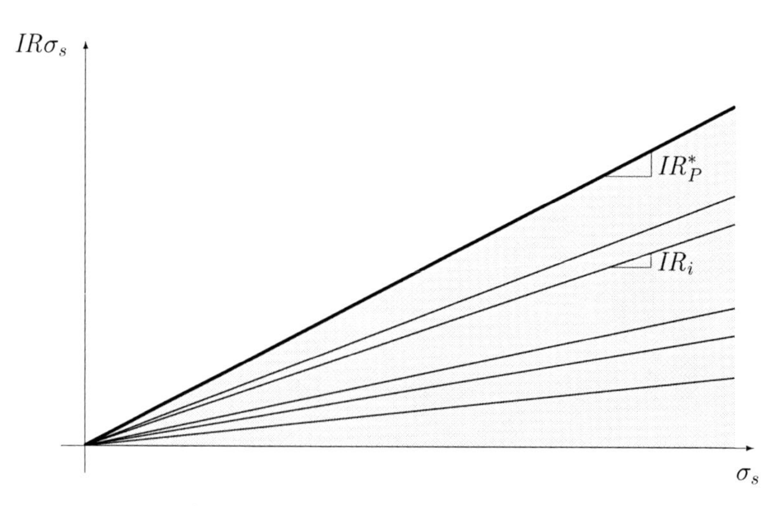

Figure 7.1: Active Risk Allocation and Active Return

Problem 7.1 (Active Risk Allocation).
Given a total active risk budget $\overline{\sigma}_{s,total}$ and correlated active returns, determine the optimal active risk allocation $\boldsymbol{\sigma}_s = (\sigma_{s_1}, \ldots, \sigma_{s_m})'$ to the m managers such that the portfolio's expected excess return is maximized:

$$\begin{aligned} \textit{objective:} \quad & \max_{\boldsymbol{\sigma}_s} \ \boldsymbol{IR}'\boldsymbol{\sigma}_s \\ \textit{constraint:} \quad & \boldsymbol{\sigma}_s'\boldsymbol{\Sigma}\boldsymbol{\sigma}_s = \overline{\sigma}^2_{s,total} \,. \end{aligned}$$

Proposition 7.2.
The optimal allocation of active risk of problem 7.1 is

$$\boldsymbol{\sigma}^*_s = \frac{\boldsymbol{\Sigma}^{-1}\boldsymbol{IR}}{\sqrt{\boldsymbol{IR}'\boldsymbol{\Sigma}^{-1}\boldsymbol{IR}}}\,\overline{\sigma}_{s,total}$$

and yields the maximum information ratio

$$IR^*_P \;=\; \sqrt{\boldsymbol{IR}'\boldsymbol{\Sigma}^{-1}\boldsymbol{IR}}\,. \tag{7.1}$$

Proof. The Lagrange function of problem 7.1 reads

$$L(\boldsymbol{\sigma}_s, \lambda) \;=\; \boldsymbol{IR}'\boldsymbol{\sigma}_s + \lambda\left(\overline{\sigma}^2_{s,\text{total}} - \boldsymbol{\sigma}_s'\boldsymbol{\Sigma}\boldsymbol{\sigma}_s\right)\,.$$

The first order conditions

$$\begin{aligned} \frac{\partial L}{\partial \boldsymbol{\sigma}_s}(\boldsymbol{\sigma}^*_s, \lambda^*) \;&=\; \boldsymbol{IR} - 2\lambda^*\boldsymbol{\Sigma}\boldsymbol{\sigma}^*_s = \boldsymbol{0} \\ \frac{\partial L}{\partial \lambda}(\boldsymbol{\sigma}^*_s, \lambda^*) \;&=\; \overline{\sigma}^2_{s,\text{total}} - \boldsymbol{\sigma}^{*\prime}_s\boldsymbol{\Sigma}\boldsymbol{\sigma}^*_s = 0 \end{aligned}$$

yield $\boldsymbol{\sigma}^*_s = \boldsymbol{\Sigma}^{-1}\boldsymbol{IR}/(2\lambda^*)$, $\lambda^* = \sqrt{\boldsymbol{IR}'\,\boldsymbol{\Sigma}^{-1}\boldsymbol{IR}}/(2\overline{\sigma}_{s,\text{total}})$ from which the stated solution $\boldsymbol{\sigma}^*_s$ results. The information ratio of this risk allocation on the overall level is

$$IR^*_P = \frac{\boldsymbol{IR}'\boldsymbol{\sigma}^*_s}{\overline{\sigma}_{s,\text{total}}} = \sqrt{\boldsymbol{IR}'\boldsymbol{\Sigma}^{-1}\boldsymbol{IR}}\,,$$

where $\boldsymbol{IR}'\boldsymbol{\sigma}^*_s = \sum_{i=1}^m IR_i\sigma^*_{s_i}$ is the total expected excess return. □

7.3 Active Risk Allocation Given a Shortfall Constraint on Active Return

Overlay risk management is specifically interested in avoiding the active return's underperformance. In case that the overlay risk management is responsible for the active risk allocation, missing certain disaster threshold returns could cause the investor to rethink the overlay mandate, e.g. if the monthly active return is less than $\tau = -10\ \%$ more than once a year. As a consequence, the active risk allocation may be subject to a further constraint on the active return's probability of falling short a threshold return. This section presents the so far unresolved solution of this risk allocation problem that is introduced by Molenkamp (2004). He proposes to add uncertainty to the information ratios and to consider confidence intervals on active returns when allocating active risk to several managers. Let IR_j, $j = 1, \ldots, m$, denote the risky information ratios. Then, the risky excess return of the ith manager equals $IR_j \sigma_{s_j}$ and the probability of the excess return falling short a threshold return τ is $P\left(\sum_{j=1}^{m} IR_j \sigma_{s_j} < \tau\right)$. For this section only, the information ratios are not assumed to be constant but to be normally distributed. The optimization problem reads:

Problem 7.3 (Active Risk Allocation Given a Shortfall Constraint).
Let $\boldsymbol{IR} = (IR_1, \ldots, IR_m)'$ *denote normally distributed information ratios with positive definite correlation matrix* $\boldsymbol{\Sigma}$ *and let* τ *denote a non-positive threshold for the active return. Given a total active risk budget* $\overline{\sigma}_{s,target}$ *and a maximum allowable threshold shortfall probability* p *of the active return, determine the optimal active risk allocation to each of the* m *strategies such that the portfolio's expected active return is maximized:*

$$\begin{array}{llll} \textit{objective:} & \max\limits_{\boldsymbol{\sigma}_s} E[\boldsymbol{IR}]'\boldsymbol{\sigma}_s & & \\ \textit{constraints:} & \boldsymbol{\sigma}_s'\boldsymbol{\Sigma}\boldsymbol{\sigma}_s & \leq & \overline{\sigma}^2_{s,target} \\ & P(\boldsymbol{IR}'\boldsymbol{\sigma}_s < \tau) & \leq & p \quad . \end{array}$$

The threshold return is set to a non-positive value, since the expected active return approaches zero for decreasing active risk and since the shortfall probability is typically constrained to a value less than 0.5. The following proposition shows that, given normally distributed information ratios, the shortfall constraint simply operates as an additional constraint on total active risk.

Proposition 7.4.
Let $\tau \leq 0$ *and* $p < \Phi\left(-\sqrt{E[\boldsymbol{IR}]'\,\boldsymbol{\Sigma}^{-1}E[\boldsymbol{IR}]}\right)$. *The optimal active risk in problem 7.3 is allocated analogously as in problem 7.1 without shortfall constraint but with optimal total active risk*

$$\overline{\sigma}^*_{s,total} = \min\left\{\overline{\sigma}_{s,target}, \frac{\tau}{\Phi^{-1}(p) + E[IR^*_P]}\right\} ,$$

where the maximum expected information ratio is

$$E[IR^*_P] = \sqrt{E[\boldsymbol{IR}]'\boldsymbol{\Sigma}^{-1}E[\boldsymbol{IR}]} .$$

Proof. Given a correlation matrix $\boldsymbol{\Sigma} \equiv (\mathrm{Corr}(IR_i, IR_j))_{i,j}$ of information ratios and a vector $\boldsymbol{\sigma}_s$ of active risks, the variance of the total excess return is the squared total fund active risk

$$\mathrm{Var}\left(\boldsymbol{IR}'\boldsymbol{\sigma}_s\right) = \boldsymbol{\sigma}_s'\boldsymbol{\Sigma}\boldsymbol{\sigma}_s = \sum_{i=1}^{m}\sum_{j=1}^{m}\sigma_{s_i}\sigma_{s_j}\mathrm{Corr}(IR_i, IR_j) .$$

The shortfall probability of the active return is

$$\begin{aligned} P\left(\boldsymbol{IR}'\boldsymbol{\sigma}_s < \tau\right) &= P\left(\frac{\boldsymbol{IR}'\boldsymbol{\sigma}_s - E[\boldsymbol{IR}]'\boldsymbol{\sigma}_s}{\sqrt{\boldsymbol{\sigma}_s'\boldsymbol{\Sigma}\boldsymbol{\sigma}_s}} < \frac{\tau - E[\boldsymbol{IR}]'\boldsymbol{\sigma}_s}{\sqrt{\boldsymbol{\sigma}_s'\boldsymbol{\Sigma}\boldsymbol{\sigma}_s}}\right) \\ &= \Phi\left(\frac{\tau - E[\boldsymbol{IR}]'\boldsymbol{\sigma}_s}{\sqrt{\boldsymbol{\sigma}_s'\boldsymbol{\Sigma}\boldsymbol{\sigma}_s}}\right) , \end{aligned}$$

where Φ denotes the standard normal distribution function. The shortfall constraint

$$p \geq P(\boldsymbol{IR}'\boldsymbol{\sigma}_s < \tau) = \Phi\left(\frac{\tau - E[\boldsymbol{IR}]'\boldsymbol{\sigma}_s}{\sqrt{\boldsymbol{\sigma}_s'\boldsymbol{\Sigma}\boldsymbol{\sigma}_s}}\right)$$

is equivalent to

$$
\begin{aligned}
0 &\geq \tau - \Phi^{-1}(p)\sqrt{\boldsymbol{\sigma}_s'\boldsymbol{\Sigma}\boldsymbol{\sigma}_s} - E[\boldsymbol{IR}]'\boldsymbol{\sigma}_s \\
&= \tau - \left(\Phi^{-1}(p) + E[IR_P]\right)\sqrt{\boldsymbol{\sigma}_s'\boldsymbol{\Sigma}\boldsymbol{\sigma}_s}\ , \qquad (7.2)
\end{aligned}
$$

where the information ratio of the portfolio is given by

$$
E[IR_P] = E[\boldsymbol{IR}]'\boldsymbol{\sigma}_s/\sqrt{\boldsymbol{\sigma}_s'\boldsymbol{\Sigma}\boldsymbol{\sigma}_s}\ .
$$

The highest expected excess return per unit active risk is achieved when the portfolio has maximum information ratio $E[IR_P^*] = \sqrt{E[\boldsymbol{IR}]'\boldsymbol{\Sigma}^{-1}E[\boldsymbol{IR}]}$ which can be derived analogously to IR_P^* given in equation (7.1). Since the condition $p < \Phi\left(-\sqrt{E[\boldsymbol{IR}]'\boldsymbol{\Sigma}^{-1}E[\boldsymbol{IR}]}\right)$ yields

$$
\begin{aligned}
0 &> \Phi^{-1}(p) + \sqrt{E[\boldsymbol{IR}]'\boldsymbol{\Sigma}^{-1}E[\boldsymbol{IR}]} = \Phi^{-1}(p) + E[IR_P^*] \\
&\geq \Phi^{-1}(p) + E[IR_P]\ ,
\end{aligned}
$$

the inequality (7.2) is equivalent to

$$
\sqrt{\boldsymbol{\sigma}_s'\boldsymbol{\Sigma}\boldsymbol{\sigma}_s} \leq \frac{\tau}{\Phi^{-1}(p) + E[IR_P]}\ .
$$

In total, the shortfall constraint can be rearranged equivalently to a constraint on total active risk. Due to the negativity of numerator and denominator, the constraint is least restrictive if the portfolio's information ratio $E[IR_P]$ is maximized, i.e. if the constraint reads $\sqrt{\boldsymbol{\sigma}_s'\boldsymbol{\Sigma}\boldsymbol{\sigma}_s} \leq \frac{\tau}{\Phi^{-1}(p)+E[IR_P^*]}$. With two constraints on total active risk, the minimum of both yields the optimal total active risk $\overline{\sigma}_{s,\text{total}}^* \equiv \min\left\{\overline{\sigma}_{s,\text{target}}, \frac{\tau}{\Phi^{-1}(p)+E[IR_P^*]}\right\}$. The optimal active risk allocation

$$
\boldsymbol{\sigma}_s^* = \frac{\boldsymbol{\Sigma}^{-1}E[\boldsymbol{IR}]}{\sqrt{E[IR_P^*]}} \min\left\{\overline{\sigma}_{s,\text{target}}, \frac{\tau}{\Phi^{-1}(p) + E[IR_P^*]}\right\}\ ,
$$

can be derived analogously as in proposition 7.2. □

7.4 Unifying Asset Allocation and Active Risk Allocation

This sections explores the combined optimization of both asset and active risk allocation. Several attempts have been made to combine asset allocation and active risk allocation. Waring, Whitney, Pirone, and Castille (2000, equation A-7) as well as Clarke, de Silva, and Wander (2002, equation 3) introduce a utility function

$$u = E[R_B] + E[R_A] - \lambda_B \sigma_B^2 - \lambda_s \sigma_s^2$$

with benchmark return R_B, benchmark excess return R_A, total benchmark risk σ_B^2 and total active risk σ_s^2. The drawback of this approach is that the penalty constants on systematic and active risk, λ_B and λ_s, need to be specified exogenously. We present a model in which the optimal total active risk is an output of the model.

The impact of active strategies on total excess return depends on the active risk and the wealth allocated to active management. If a portfolio manager is assigned fund weight x_i and active risk σ_{s_i} for his strategy with information ratio IR_i, the excess return contribution to total active return is $x_i IR_i \sigma_{s_i}$. The simultaneous optimization of x_i and σ_{s_i} is tricky due to the product of x_i and σ_{s_i}. In order to solve the optimization problem, we first consider a related problem. We assume that the active strategies are applied on total fund weight 1 and contribute $IR_i \sigma_{s_i}$ each to the total excess return. The expected portfolio return is the sum of weighted asset returns (or asset class returns) $\sum_{i=1}^{n} \mu_i x_i = \boldsymbol{\mu}'\mathbf{x}$ and active returns $\sum_{j=1}^{m} IR_j \sigma_{s_j} = \boldsymbol{IR}'\boldsymbol{\sigma}_s$. In the following, the total portfolio risk is minimized for a prespecified level μ_P of expected total portfolio return.

Problem 7.5 (Simultaneous Asset and Active Risk Allocation).
Given that m active strategies are applied on total fund weight 1, determine the optimal asset allocation $\mathbf{x} = (x_1, \ldots, x_n)'$ to n assets (or asset classes) and the active risk allocation $\boldsymbol{\sigma}_s = (\sigma_{s_1}, \ldots, \sigma_{s_m})'$ such that total portfolio risk is minimized for a specified expected portfolio return μ_P:

$$\begin{array}{lll} \textit{objective:} & \min_{\mathbf{x},\boldsymbol{\sigma}_s} \mathbf{x}'\boldsymbol{V}\mathbf{x} + \boldsymbol{\sigma}_s'\boldsymbol{\Sigma}\boldsymbol{\sigma}_s & \\ \textit{constraints:} & \mathbf{x}'\boldsymbol{\mu} + \boldsymbol{IR}'\boldsymbol{\sigma}_s & = \mu_P \\ & \mathbf{x}'\mathbf{1} & = 1 \quad . \end{array}$$

Closed form solutions can be derived under the assumptions 2.1 (frictionless market), 2.2 (risky assets), and 7.1 (active strategies). By assumption 7.1, active returns are uncorrelated with asset returns and covariance terms do not appear in the total portfolio risk $\sigma_P^2 = \text{Var}(R_B + R_A) = \mathbf{x}'\boldsymbol{V}\mathbf{x} + \boldsymbol{\sigma}_s'\boldsymbol{\Sigma}\boldsymbol{\sigma}_s$. The constraint on the expected return of the type $\mathbf{x}'\boldsymbol{\mu} + \boldsymbol{IR}'\boldsymbol{\sigma}_s = \mu_P$ is linear in both variables x_i and σ_{s_j}. The problem is quadratic with a quadratic objective function and linear constraints. The asset returns might also stand for benchmark returns of asset classes and the asset allocation would be an asset class allocation in this case.

Proposition 7.6.
Given a target expected portfolio return μ_P with $\mu_P \geq \mu_{\text{MVP}}$, the optimal total active risk budget for problem 7.5 is

$$\sigma_{s,total} = \frac{\mu_P - \mu_{\text{MVP}}}{d + (IR_P^*)^2} IR_P^* \tag{7.3}$$

and the maximum information ratio is $IR_P^* \equiv \sqrt{\boldsymbol{IR}'\boldsymbol{\Sigma}^{-1}\boldsymbol{IR}}$. The optimal portfolio is achieved with the asset allocation

$$\mathbf{x} = \boldsymbol{V}^{-1}\left(\frac{\sigma_{s,total}}{IR_P^*}(\boldsymbol{\mu} - \mu_{\text{MVP}}\mathbf{1}) + \sigma_{\text{MVP}}^2\mathbf{1}\right) \tag{7.4}$$

and the active risk allocation

$$\boldsymbol{\sigma}_s = \frac{\boldsymbol{\Sigma}^{-1}\boldsymbol{IR}}{IR_P^*}\sigma_{s,total} \; . \tag{7.5}$$

The total portfolio risk is

$$\sigma_P^2 = \sigma_{\mathrm{MVP}}^2 + \frac{(\mu_P - \mu_{\mathrm{MVP}})^2}{d + (IR_P^*)^2} \,. \tag{7.6}$$

Proof. The Lagrange function of problem 7.5 is

$$L(\mathbf{x}, \boldsymbol{\sigma}_s, \lambda_1, \lambda_2) = \mathbf{x}'\boldsymbol{V}\mathbf{x} + \boldsymbol{\sigma}_s'\boldsymbol{\Sigma}\boldsymbol{\sigma}_s + \lambda_1 \left(\mu_P - \mathbf{x}'\boldsymbol{\mu} - \boldsymbol{IR}'\boldsymbol{\sigma}_s\right) + \lambda_2 \left(1 - \mathbf{x}'\mathbf{1}\right)$$

and the first order conditions are

$$\frac{\partial L}{\partial \mathbf{x}} = 2\boldsymbol{V}\mathbf{x} - \lambda_1\boldsymbol{\mu} - \lambda_2\mathbf{1} = \mathbf{0} \tag{7.7}$$

$$\frac{\partial L}{\partial \boldsymbol{\sigma}_s} = 2\boldsymbol{\Sigma}\boldsymbol{\sigma}_s - \lambda_1\boldsymbol{IR} = \mathbf{0} \tag{7.8}$$

$$\frac{\partial L}{\partial \lambda_1} = \mu_P - \mathbf{x}'\boldsymbol{\mu} - \boldsymbol{\sigma}_s'\boldsymbol{IR} = 0 \tag{7.9}$$

$$\frac{\partial L}{\partial \lambda_2} = 1 - \mathbf{x}'\mathbf{1} = 0 \,. \tag{7.10}$$

Since the covariance matrix $\boldsymbol{V}$ is invertible, equation (7.7) can be solved for the asset allocation vector

$$\mathbf{x} = \frac{1}{2}\boldsymbol{V}^{-1}\left(\boldsymbol{\mu}\ \mathbf{1}\right)\begin{pmatrix}\lambda_1\\ \lambda_2\end{pmatrix} \,. \tag{7.11}$$

In order to obtain the Lagrange multipliers λ_1 and λ_2, we first insert $\mathbf{x}$ in equation (7.10)

$$0 = 1 - \mathbf{x}'\mathbf{1} = 1 - \frac{1}{2}\lambda_1\mathbf{1}'\boldsymbol{V}^{-1}\boldsymbol{\mu} - \frac{1}{2}\lambda_2\mathbf{1}'\boldsymbol{V}^{-1}\mathbf{1}$$

and rearrange to

$$\lambda_2 = 2\frac{1 - \frac{1}{2}\lambda_1\mathbf{1}'\boldsymbol{V}^{-1}\boldsymbol{\mu}}{\mathbf{1}'\boldsymbol{V}^{-1}\mathbf{1}} \,.$$

Using the expressions $\mathbf{x}$ and λ_2 as well as $\boldsymbol{\sigma}_s = \frac{\lambda_1}{2}\boldsymbol{\Sigma}^{-1}\boldsymbol{IR}$ from equation (7.8), equation (7.9) yields

$$\begin{aligned} 0 &= \mu_P - \mathbf{x}'\boldsymbol{\mu} - \boldsymbol{\sigma}_s'\boldsymbol{IR} \\ &= \mu_P - \left(\frac{1}{2}\lambda_1\boldsymbol{\mu}'\boldsymbol{V}^{-1}\boldsymbol{\mu} + \frac{1}{2}\lambda_2\boldsymbol{\mu}\boldsymbol{V}^{-1}\mathbf{1}\right) - \frac{1}{2}\lambda_1\boldsymbol{IR}'\boldsymbol{\Sigma}^{-1}\boldsymbol{IR} \\ &= \mu_P - \frac{1}{2}\lambda_1\left(\boldsymbol{\mu}'\boldsymbol{V}^{-1}\boldsymbol{\mu} + \boldsymbol{IR}'\boldsymbol{\Sigma}^{-1}\boldsymbol{IR}\right) - \frac{1 - \frac{1}{2}\lambda_1\mathbf{1}'\boldsymbol{V}^{-1}\boldsymbol{\mu}}{\mathbf{1}'\boldsymbol{V}^{-1}\mathbf{1}}\boldsymbol{\mu}'\boldsymbol{V}^{-1}\mathbf{1} \end{aligned}$$

which can be solved for λ_1

$$\lambda_1 = 2\frac{\mu_P\mathbf{1}'\boldsymbol{V}^{-1}\mathbf{1} - \boldsymbol{\mu}'\boldsymbol{V}^{-1}\mathbf{1}}{\left(\boldsymbol{\mu}'\boldsymbol{V}^{-1}\boldsymbol{\mu} + \boldsymbol{IR}'\boldsymbol{\Sigma}^{-1}\boldsymbol{IR}\right)\mathbf{1}'\boldsymbol{V}^{-1}\mathbf{1} - \mathbf{1}\boldsymbol{V}^{-1}\boldsymbol{\mu}\boldsymbol{\mu}'\boldsymbol{V}^{-1}\mathbf{1}} .$$

The expressions for the Lagrange multipliers can be rearranged with the information matrix elements $a = \boldsymbol{\mu}'\boldsymbol{V}^{-1}\boldsymbol{\mu}$, $b = \boldsymbol{\mu}'\boldsymbol{V}^{-1}\mathbf{1}$, $c = \boldsymbol{\mu}'\boldsymbol{V}^{-1}\boldsymbol{\mu}$, with $d \equiv a - b^2/c$, and with the maximum information ratio $IR_P^* = \sqrt{\boldsymbol{IR}'\boldsymbol{\Sigma}^{-1}\boldsymbol{IR}}$ to

$$\begin{aligned} \lambda_1 &= 2\frac{\mu_P c - b}{(a + IR_P^*)c - b^2} = 2\frac{\mu_P - \frac{b}{c}}{a - \frac{b^2}{c} + IR_P^*} = 2\frac{\mu_P - \mu_{\mathrm{MVP}}}{d + IR_P^*} \\ \lambda_2 &= 2\left(\frac{1}{c} - \frac{1}{2}\lambda_1\frac{b}{c}\right) = 2\left(\sigma_{\mathrm{MVP}}^2 - \frac{\mu_P - \mu_{\mathrm{MVP}}}{d + IR_P^*}\mu_{\mathrm{MVP}}\right) . \end{aligned}$$

Inserting λ_1 and λ_2 in equations (7.11) and (7.8) yields the optimal asset and risk allocations

$$\begin{aligned} \mathbf{x} &= \boldsymbol{V}^{-1}(\boldsymbol{\mu}\ \mathbf{1})\begin{pmatrix} \frac{\mu_P - \mu_{\mathrm{MVP}}}{d + (IR_P^*)^2} \\ \sigma_{\mathrm{MVP}}^2 - \frac{\mu_P - \mu_{\mathrm{MVP}}}{d + (IR_P^*)^2}\mu_{\mathrm{MVP}} \end{pmatrix} \\ &= \boldsymbol{V}^{-1}\left(\frac{\mu_P - \mu_{\mathrm{MVP}}}{d + (IR_P^*)^2}(\boldsymbol{\mu} - \mu_{\mathrm{MVP}}\mathbf{1}) + \sigma_{\mathrm{MVP}}^2\mathbf{1}\right) \\ &= \boldsymbol{V}^{-1}\left(\frac{\sigma_{s,\mathrm{total}}}{IR_P^*}(\boldsymbol{\mu} - \mu_{\mathrm{MVP}}\mathbf{1}) + \sigma_{\mathrm{MVP}}^2\mathbf{1}\right) \\ \boldsymbol{\sigma}_s &= \frac{\mu_P - \mu_{\mathrm{MVP}}}{d + (IR_P^*)^2}\boldsymbol{\Sigma}^{-1}\boldsymbol{IR} = \frac{\boldsymbol{\Sigma}^{-1}\boldsymbol{IR}}{IR_P^*}\sigma_{s,\mathrm{total}} , \end{aligned}$$

where the total active risk

$$\sigma_{s,\mathrm{total}} = \sqrt{\boldsymbol{\sigma}_s'\boldsymbol{\Sigma}\boldsymbol{\sigma}_s} = \frac{\mu_P - \mu_{\mathrm{MVP}}}{d + (IR_P^*)^2}IR_P$$

helps to simplify the formulas. Using the elements of the information matrix, the total portfolio risk is

$$\begin{aligned}\sigma_P^2 &= \mathbf{x}'\boldsymbol{V}\mathbf{x} + \sigma_{s,\text{total}}^2 \\ &= \frac{\sigma_{s,\text{total}}^2}{(IR_P^*)^2}\left(\boldsymbol{\mu}'\boldsymbol{V}^{-1}\boldsymbol{\mu} - \frac{b^2}{c^2}\mathbf{1}'\boldsymbol{V}^{-1}\mathbf{1}\right) + \frac{1}{c^2}\mathbf{1}'\boldsymbol{V}^{-1}\mathbf{1} + \sigma_{s,\text{total}}^2 \\ &= \sigma_{\text{MVP}}^2 + \frac{(\mu_P - \mu_{\text{MVP}})^2}{d + (IR_P^*)^2}\,.\end{aligned}$$

□

The optimal asset allocation and active risk allocation depend on the optimal active risk which is derived endogenously. When the optimal total active risk is known, the optimal active risk allocation can be implemented separately from the asset allocation. This is a result of the optimization and it has not been assumed, as it is usually the case in other models of active risk allocation.

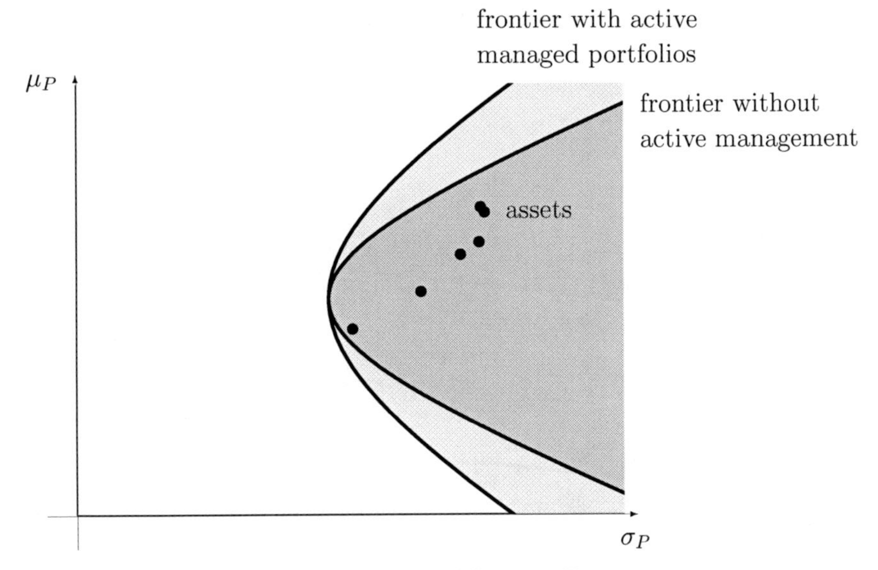

Figure 7.2: Active and Passive Frontier

Adding active management extends the mean-variance frontier of the passive portfolio selection presented in chapter 2, as illustrated by figure 7.2. When the expected portfolio return is kept constant, the total risk of a passive frontier portfolio is reduced by the absolute amount

$$\begin{aligned}\sigma^2_{P_{\text{passive}}} - \sigma^2_{P_{\text{active}}} &= \frac{(\mu_P - \mu_{\text{MVP}})^2}{d} - \frac{(\mu_P - \mu_{\text{MVP}})^2}{d + (IR^*_P)^2} \\ &= \frac{(\mu_P - \mu_{\text{MVP}})^2 (IR^*_P)^2}{d^2 + d(IR^*_P)^2},\end{aligned}$$

where equations (2.11) and (7.6) are used. The relative reduction of total risk is

$$\frac{\sigma^2_{P_{\text{active}}} - \sigma^2_{P_{\text{passive}}}}{\sigma^2_{P_{\text{passive}}}} = -\frac{(IR^*_P)^2}{d + (IR^*_P)^2}.$$

Equation (7.6) can be rearranged to a hyperbola equation

$$\frac{\sigma^2_P}{\sigma^2_{\text{MVP}}} - \frac{(\mu_P - \mu_{\text{MVP}})^2}{(d + (IR^*_P)^2)\sigma^2_{\text{MVP}}} = 1$$

which is similar to the hyperbola equation (2.10) for frontier portfolios without active management; only d is replaced by $d + (IR^*_P)^2$ in the second denominator. The slopes of the hyperbola's asymptotes are then $\pm\sqrt{d + (IR^*_P)^2}$. An alternative problem is that the expected portfolio return is maximized if a total risk budget of passive and active risk, σ^2_P, is given. The solution is given by proposition 7.6 with expected portfolio return

$$\mu_P = \mu_{\text{MVP}} + \sqrt{(d + (IR^*_P)^2)(\sigma^2_P - \sigma^2_{\text{MVP}})}.$$

We can now consider the case that one active strategy is implemented in each asset class, i.e. the numbers of asset classes and active strategies are identical, $m = n$. If the ith manager is assigned fund weight x_i and active risk σ_{s_i}, then the active managed asset class contributes $x_i\,(\mu_i + IR_i\sigma_{s_i})$ to the total expected portfolio return $\sum_{i=1}^{n} x_i(\mu_i + IR_i\sigma_{s_i})$. The constraint $\sum_{i=1}^{n} x_i(\mu_i + IR_i\sigma_{s_i}) = \mu_P$ on the expected return is not linear due to the product of the variables x_i and σ_{s_i}. Since an inequality condition $\sum_{i=1}^{n} x_i(\mu_i + IR_i\sigma_{s_i}) \geq \mu_P$ is a concave constraint, the Karush-Kuhn-Tucker conditions cannot be used to derive the solution. However, the solution of this problem can be derived by making use of the assumption 7.1 that scaling of an active strategy is possible without loss of information ratio. The optimal risk allocation of proposition 7.6 is based on total fund level. The active risk allocation can also be expressed as a more aggressive implementation of the strategies that are each restricted to an asset class weight x_i, $i = 1, \ldots, n$. If the ith manager is responsible to generate an expected return $x_i\mu_i + IR_i\sigma_{s_i} = x_i(\mu_i + IR_i\sigma_{s_i}/x_i)$ for the total fund, the ith strategy has to have the active risk σ_{s_i}/x_i and yield an expected excess return $IR_i\sigma_{s_i}/x_i$ for the assigned asset allocation x_i. The risk allocation σ_{s_i} and excess return contribution $IR_i\sigma_{s_i}$ on total fund level remain unchanged. Summarizing, we have

Proposition 7.7 (Three Step Asset Class and Active Risk Allocation). *The simultaneous optimization of asset class weight x_i and active risk allocation σ_{s_i} to the ith asset class manager can be separated in three steps:*

First, determine the optimal total active risk budget using equation (7.3).

Second, allocate asset class weights according to equation (7.4).

Third, allocate the active risk σ_{s_i}/x_i to the manager of the ith asset class, where x_i and σ_{s_i} are given by equations (7.4) and (7.5), respectively.

Example 7.8 (Active Risk for Fixed Income and Equity Portfolios).

In this example, overlay managers want to determine the optimal active risks and weights for a portfolio consisting of a fixed income fund and an equity fund. The expected returns and volatilities of the benchmarks and the information ratios of the fund managers are

	μ_{B_i}	σ_{B_i}	IR_i
fund 1	0.04	0.03	0.5
fund 2	0.10	0.14	0.4

The correlation of the fund's benchmark returns is $\rho_{B_1,B_2} = 0.2$ and the active strategies are uncorrelated. What is the optimal allocation of fund weights and active risks that maximizes the expected portfolio return given that total portfolio volatility is restricted to $\sigma_P = 0.05$?

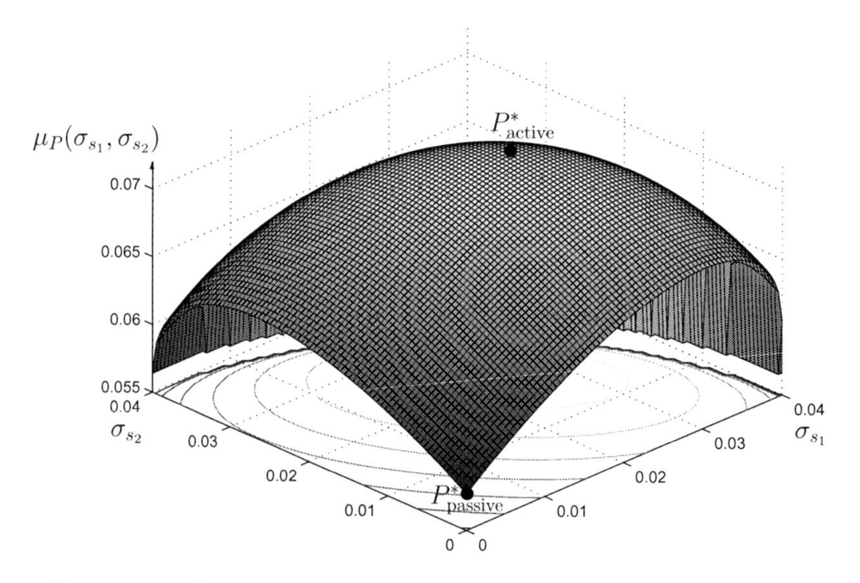

Figure 7.3: Active Risks and Expected Portfolio Return When Total Risk is Fixed

Figure 7.3 displays the expected portfolio return as a function of active risks when total portfolio risk is restricted to $\sigma_P = 0.05$. The optimal total active risk is $\sigma^*_{s,\text{total}} = 0.03303$ and the optimal solutions without and with active management are:

portfolio	x_1^*	x_2^*	$\sigma^*_{s_1}$	$\sigma^*_{s_2}$	μ_P^*	σ_P
P^*_{passive}	0.7052	0.2948	0	0	0.05769	0.0500
P^*_{active}	0.8323	0.1677	0.02579	0.02064	0.07121	0.0500

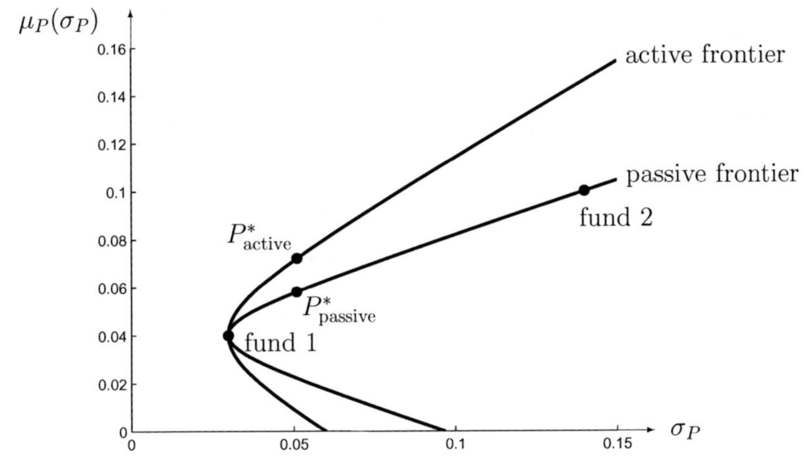

Figure 7.4: Portfolios with and without Active Management

In the case of uncorrelated active returns, the optimal active risks and information ratios are proportional: $IR_1/\sigma^*_{s_1} = IR_2/\sigma^*_{s_2} = 19.3845$. The total weight x_2 of the riskier fund 2 is smaller in the optimal active portfolio compared to the passive portfolio, since risk is moved from passive to active risk. If active management is implemented on fund level, funds 1 and 2 are assigned active risks $\sigma^*_{s_1}/x_1^* = 0.0310$ and $\sigma^*_{s_2}/x_2^* = 0.1231$, respectively. Figure 7.4 illustrates the mean-variance-frontier of passive and active managed portfolios.

7.5 Safety First Approach for Decentralized Investing

This section derives the optimal total active risk for investors that pursue the safety first approach when active strategies are available. In contrast to the previous section, the optimal asset allocation does not depend on the optimal amount of total active risk. Instead, adding active strategies enhances the optimal portfolio while the optimal passive allocation remains unchanged. The results also apply if the Sharpe ratio is maximized.

For the remainder of this chapter, we derive closed form solutions under the assumptions 2.1 (frictionless market), 2.2 (risky assets), 2.4 (normally distributed asset returns), 7.1 (active strategies), and the following

Assumption 7.2 (Normally Distributed Active Returns).
The excess returns of the active strategies are normally distributed.

Problem 7.9 (Safety First).
Determine the optimal asset allocation and active risk allocation such that the probability of falling short a target return τ is minimized:

$$\begin{array}{ll} \textit{objective:} & \min_{\mathbf{x},\boldsymbol{\sigma}_s} P(R_P < \tau) \\ \textit{constraint:} & \mathbf{x}'\mathbf{1} = 1 \quad . \end{array}$$

Proposition 7.10.
Let $\tau < \mu_{\text{MVP}}$. The minimum shortfall probability in problem 7.9 is achieved with total active risk

$$\sigma^*_{s,total} = \sigma^2_{\text{MVP}} \frac{IR^*_P}{\mu_{\text{MVP}} - \tau}$$

and the active risk allocation given in equation (7.5). The asset allocation is identical to the safety first solution $P^*_{passive}$ without active management given in proposition 2.6. The portfolio's expected return and total portfolio *risk are*

$$\mu_P^* = \frac{a - b\tau + (IR_P^*)^2}{b - c\tau} = \mu_{P^*_{\text{passive}}} + IR_P^* \, \sigma^*_{s,total} \tag{7.12}$$

$$\sigma_P^{*\,2} = \frac{a - 2b\tau + c\tau^2 + (IR_P^*)^2}{(b - c\tau)^2} = \sigma^2_{P^*_{\text{passive}}} + \sigma^{*\,2}_{s,total} \, . \tag{7.13}$$

Proof. Analogously to the derivations in section 2.3, the minimum shortfall probability satisfies the condition

$$\frac{\partial \frac{\mu_P - \tau}{\sigma_P}}{\partial \mu_P}(\mu_P^*) = \frac{1}{\sigma_P} - \frac{(\mu_P - \mu_{\text{MVP}})(\mu_P - \tau)}{(d + (IR_P^*)^2)\sigma_P^3} = 0 \, ,$$

where σ_P is given in equation (7.6) and depends on μ_P. This condition yields

$$\mu_P^* = \frac{a - b\tau + (IR_P^*)^2}{b - c\tau}$$

which also satisfies the condition

$$\begin{aligned}
\frac{\partial^2 \frac{\mu_P - \tau}{\sigma_P}}{\partial \mu_P^2}(\mu_P^*) &= -\frac{\mu_{\text{MVP}} - \tau}{(d + (IR_P^*)^2)\left(\frac{(IR_P^*)^2 + a - 2b\tau + c\tau^2}{(b - c\tau)^2}\right)^{3/2}} \\
&= -\frac{1}{c^4}\frac{(\mu_{\text{MVP}} - \tau)^4}{(d + (IR_P^*)^2)\left((IR_P^*)^2/c + a/c - 2\mu_{\text{MVP}}\tau + \tau^2\right)^{3/2}} < 0 \, ,
\end{aligned}$$

where $\det(\boldsymbol{A}) = ac - b^2 > 0 \Rightarrow a/c > (b/c)^2 = \mu^2_{\text{MVP}}$ is used. This expected return yields the maximum of the shortfall slope and the minimum of the shortfall probability according to equation (2.18). It is also used to calculate the optimal total active risk. Equation (7.6) yields the total portfolio risk. The alternative expressions of expected return and variance in equations (7.12) and (7.13) can be derived with the safety first solution P^*_{passive} without active management given in proposition 2.6. The expected return and variance of the asset allocation can also be derived by

$$\begin{aligned}
\boldsymbol{\mu}'\mathbf{x} &= \boldsymbol{\mu}'\boldsymbol{V}^{-1}\frac{\boldsymbol{\mu} - \tau\mathbf{1}}{\mu_{\text{MVP}} - \tau}\sigma^2_{\text{MVP}} = \frac{a - b\tau}{b - c\tau} \\
\mathbf{x}'\boldsymbol{V}\mathbf{x} &= \frac{\boldsymbol{\mu} - \tau\mathbf{1}}{b - c\tau}\boldsymbol{V}^{-1}\frac{\boldsymbol{\mu} - \tau\mathbf{1}}{b - c\tau} = \frac{a - 2b\tau + c\tau^2}{(b - c\tau)^2} \, ,
\end{aligned}$$

where the elements of the information matrix and equation (7.4) are used. Since a passive frontier portfolio is identified uniquely by its expected return and variance, the vector $\mathbf{x}$ is the composition of the passive safety first portfolio of proposition 2.6. □

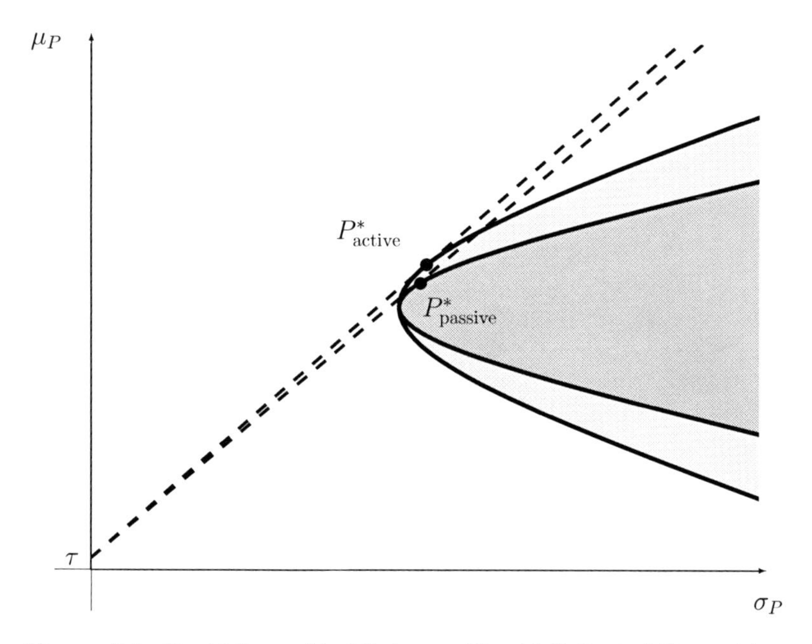

Figure 7.5: Portfolios with Minimum Shortfall Probability with and without Active Management

Figure 7.5 illustrates the optimal active and passive solution of the safety first problem. In contrast to the previous section, the allocation of fund weights is independent of the total active risk and is identical to the case of the safety first approach without active management. Adding active management to the safety first approach does not influence the strategic asset allocation. However, it increases the expected return of the portfolio by the absolute amount

$$\mu_P^* - \mu_{P_{\text{passive}}} = \frac{a - b\tau + (IR_P^*)^2}{b - c\tau} - \frac{a - b\tau}{b - c\tau} = \frac{(IR_P^*)^2}{b - c\tau} = \sigma_{\text{MVP}}^2 \frac{(IR_P^*)^2}{\mu_{\text{MVP}} - \tau},$$

where equation (2.19) provides the expected return of the shortfall probability minimizing portfolio without active management. Proposition 7.10 and above results are also useful for investors that maximize the Sharpe ratio. As is shown in section 2.3, the threshold return only needs to be replaced by the riskless rate. When maximizing the Sharpe ratio, the results are also valid without the normal distribution assumptions 2.4 (normally distributed asset returns) and 7.2 (normally distributed active returns). Overlay portfolio management can include active strategies to enhance the safety first approach as well as the portfolio's Sharpe ratio without changing the strategic allocation.

Similar conclusions are derived by Treynor and Black (1973) in a different model set-up. They rely on a one-factor market model with uncorrelated residual returns of assets. Superior information on the expected residual returns enable the investor to extend the passive frontier that is given in market equilibrium. In contrast to above model, active return is not generated with self-financing strategies but with allocation of wealth to single securities which is not necessarily self-financing. As a second minor point, active returns are not allowed to be correlated. Furthermore, they do not consider explicit active risk allocation but allocation of wealth. The most important difference however is that they *assume* that the optimal passive allocation is given by the market portfolio, while we show *by optimization* that asset allocation and active risk allocation can be optimized separately. In the special case of $\tau = r_f$, our optimal passive portfolio results to be a tangency portfolio which corresponds to their market portfolio in market equilibrium. The following section addresses a problem for which asset allocation and active risk allocation cannot be separated and both depend on the optimal amount of active risk.

7.6 Value at Risk Optimization for Decentralized Investing

This section presents the optimal asset allocation and active risk allocation for financial institutions that want to minimize a portfolio's Value at Risk. Figure 7.6 illustrates the optimal solution with and without active management.

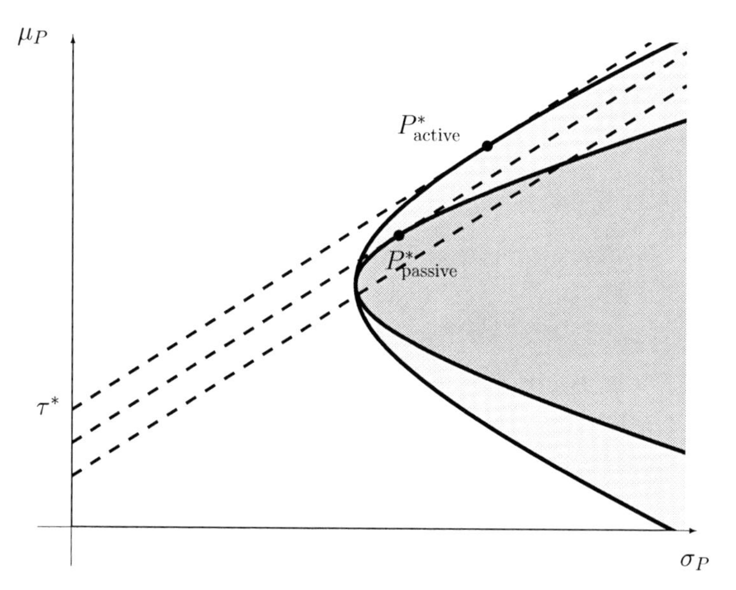

Figure 7.6: Portfolios with Minimum VaR with and without Active Management

Problem 7.11 (Minimize VaR).
Given a shortfall probability p, determine the optimal asset allocation and active risk allocation such that the threshold return is maximized:

$$\begin{aligned} \textit{objective:} \quad & \max_{\mathbf{x},\boldsymbol{\sigma}_s} \tau \\ \textit{constraint:} \quad & P(R_P < \tau) = p \,. \end{aligned}$$

Adding active management yields formulas that are similar to those of the passive case; the only difference is that d is replaced by $d + (IR^*_P)^2$ in proposition 2.8. This stems from the extension of the efficient frontier. As in section 7.4 and in contrast to the previous section 7.5, the optimal strategic asset allocation depends on the optimal total active risk.

Proposition 7.12.
Let $p < \Phi\left(-\sqrt{d + (IR^*_P)^2}\right)$. The maximum threshold return of problem 7.11 is

$$\tau^* = \mu_{\mathrm{MVP}} - \sqrt{m_p^2 - d - (IR^*_P)^2}\,\sigma_{\mathrm{MVP}} \,.$$

It is achieved with total active risk

$$\sigma^*_{s,total} = \frac{IR^*_P}{\sqrt{m_p^2 - d - (IR^*_P)^2}}\,\sigma_{\mathrm{MVP}}$$

and the asset and active risk allocation given in equations (7.4) and (7.5). The active portfolio's expected return and standard deviation are

$$\mu^*_P = \mu_{\mathrm{MVP}} + \frac{d + (IR^*_P)^2}{\sqrt{m_p^2 - d - (IR^*_P)^2}}\,\sigma_{\mathrm{MVP}}$$

$$\sigma^*_P = \frac{m_p}{\sqrt{m_p^2 - d - (IR^*_P)^2}}\,\sigma_{\mathrm{MVP}} \,,$$

where $m_p \equiv \Phi^{-1}(1-p)$.

Proof. This proof is analogous to the proof of proposition 2.8. If the threshold return is maximized, the optimal active portfolio is on the efficient frontier of active portfolios. Solving the shortfall line equation $\mu_P = \tau + m_p\sigma_P$ for the threshold return and using equation (7.6) yields the threshold return τ as a function of the expected return of the frontier portfolio

$$\tau = \mu_P - m_p\sigma_P = \mu_P - m_p\sqrt{\sigma^2_{\mathrm{MVP}} + \frac{(\mu_P - \mu_{\mathrm{MVP}})^2}{d + (IR^*_P)^2}} \,.$$

The first order condition for the optimal expected return

$$\frac{\partial \tau}{\partial \mu_P}(\mu_P^*) = 1 - \frac{m_p(\mu_P - \mu_{\text{MVP}})}{(d + (IR_P^*)^2)\sqrt{\sigma_{\text{MVP}}^2 + \frac{(\mu_P - \mu_{\text{MVP}})^2}{d + (IR_P^*)^2}}} = 0$$

has solution

$$\mu_P^* = \mu_{\text{MVP}} + \frac{d + (IR_P^*)^2}{\sqrt{m_p^2 - d - (IR_P^*)^2}}\sigma_{\text{MVP}} ,$$

which also satisfies the maximum condition

$$\frac{\partial^2 \tau}{\partial \mu_P^2}(\mu_P^*) = -\frac{(m_p^2 - d - (IR_P^*)^2)^{3/2}}{m_p^2(d + (IR_P^*)^2)\sigma_{\text{MVP}}} < 0 .$$

The total portfolio risk can be calculated with equation (7.6). Using equation (7.6) and the optimal expected return, the maximum threshold can be simplified to

$$\tau^* = \mu_P^* - m_p\sigma_P^* = \mu_{\text{MVP}} - \sqrt{m_p^2 - d - (IR_P^*)^2}\,\sigma_{\text{MVP}} .$$

Equation (7.3) yields the optimal total active risk for the optimal expected return

$$\sigma_{s,\text{total}}^* = \frac{IR_P^*}{\sqrt{m_p^2 - d - (IR_P^*)^2}}\sigma_{\text{MVP}} .$$

□

Chapter 8

Conclusion

The delegation of financial investment decisions has gained much attention recently by investment companies as well as by academia. The efficient organization of the investment process within investment companies is a complex interplay of delegation of investment authority, portfolio management, and risk management. Private investors delegate investment decisions on the majority of wealth to financial professionals. Despite the obvious relevance of the delegation process, a standard model of delegated investing has not evolved so far. This dissertation sets up a model framework of delegating investment decisions to one or several agents and derives implications on the optimal asset allocation and optimal risk allocation. Relevant elements from portfolio theory and principal-agent theory are combined to a holistic theory of delegated investing.

A framework of delegated portfolio selection requires at least one principal who delegates and one agent who composes the portfolio. In many situations, the principal's risk-return preferences may be best represented by an absolute objective such as the classical mean-variance criterion or the safety first approach of minimizing the shortfall probability. The agent's contribution to portfolio performance is typically measured against a benchmark's performance. Restrictions on deviations from the benchmark composition lead to portfolio reallocations relative to the benchmark. This benchmark-relative portfolio selection differs essentially from the absolute portfolio selection in the tradition of Markowitz. However, the principal may not be able to force the agent to implement absolute portfolio selection but may have to rely on benchmark-relative portfolio selection.

The principal's objective is mainly established by defining a strategic benchmark. The senior management of an investment company can try to improve the portfolio's performance with active management and use risk limits to constrain the active management's deviations from the benchmark allocation. Allocating active risk aims at allowing for the right amount of flexibility in active management. A principal whose objective is to implement the safety first approach should consider the agent's benchmark-relative portfolio selection. In our model framework, the principal can allocate an optimal active risk budget such that the delegated portfolio selection is optimal among all benchmark-relative portfolios. This second-best solution can be improved further with an additional constraint on portfolio beta. Given optimal constraints on active risk and portfolio beta, the second-best solution coincides with the first-best solution which is the best portfolio among all possible portfolios.

Investment authority is typically delegated from a less informed to a more informed person or from a person who oversees several areas to a person who is specialized in one area. The fundamental question is: Which information is essential for delegating? Given that the delegation is controlled via active risk constraints, the derived formulas of active risk limits reveal the information that is sufficient for an optimal risk allocation. The principal does not need to know the agent's estimates of expected returns and covariances. Instead, the expected return of the MVP and the expected return and volatility of the benchmark-relative portfolios that the agent composes is sufficient for the optimal active risk constraint. The agent can disclose this data without the delegation becoming dispensable.

With additional information on mean and variance of frontier portfolios, the principal is able to additionally constrain portfolio beta such that the manager chooses a portfolio that is the first-best solution.

An optimal allocation of active risk and beta risk enhances the results of the delegated portfolio selection. Changes in the agent's estimates of the assets' expected returns or covariances affect the agent's reallocation decision, but not necessarily the principal's optimal risk allocation. The risk budgets need not be adapted as long as the agent's information ratio and fundamental market conditions remain unchanged. In the model, these market fundamentals are the mean-variance characteristics of frontier portfolios that are given by an hyperbola in mean-volatility space. The implications of market-wide increasing expected returns on the optimal active risk allocation can be analyzed with the derived formulas by shifting the hyperbola upwards. General changes in volatilities and necessary adjustments of the active risk allocation can be analyzed by shifting the hyperbola sidewards. The comparative analysis does not need to consider single securities, but only the general location and shape of the hyperbola. It allows to analyze necessary changes of the optimal risk allocation when market conditions change in general.

We also study the simultaneous portfolio selection and active risk allocation when active management is delegated to multiple managers. We refuse the assumption that asset allocation and active management can be optimized in general independently of each other. The optimal asset allocation depends on the optimal total active risk if the VaR is to be minimized as well as if the portfolio volatility is to be minimized at a given expected return level. In order to avoid suboptimal solutions, the optimal total active risk has to be determined first. Then, asset allocation and active risk allocation can be optimized separately. However, we have shown by optimization that the assumption is valid if the objective is to maximize the Sharpe ratio or to minimize the shortfall probability. In these two cases, the asset allocation and the active risk allocation can be optimized separately: The optimal asset allocation is identical to the allocation without active management, and the active management can be optimized independently and be added to the portfolio.

To summarize, the following results are the main contributions of this dissertation: We present a theory of delegated investing that combines the investor's absolute objective with the active management's benchmark-relative objective. The investor can use the strategic asset allocation to set up a benchmark for the delegated portfolio selection and improve it with active management. The optimal allocation of active risk provides the active portfolio managers with the right extend of flexibility to enhance the strategic decision with active strategies. Closed form solutions of the optimal active risk allocation are derived for the safety first approach, for maximizing the Sharpe ratio as well as for minimizing the portfolio's VaR or variance. Closed form solutions are also derived for the simultaneous asset allocation and active risk allocation to multiple active strategies. Asset allocation and active risk allocation can be implemented separately for the safety first approach as well as for maximizing the Sharpe ratio. However, the optimal asset allocation depends on total active risk when minimizing the portfolio's VaR or volatility. When all investors delegate investment decisions and control the delegated portfolio selection with respect to the safety first approach or the Sharpe ratio, the expected asset returns depend on the objective functions of both investors and portfolio managers, and they are described by a two-factor model in market equilibrium.

Bibliography

Admati, Anat R., and Paul Pfleiderer, 1997, Does It All Add Up? Benchmarks and the Compensation of Active Portfolio Managers, *The Journal of Business* 70, 323–350.

Allen, Franklin, 2001, Do Financial Institutions Matter?, *The Journal of Finance* 56, 1165–1175.

Ambachtsheer, Keith, 2005, Beyond Portfolio Theory: The Next Frontier, *Financial Analysts Journal* 61, 29–33.

Ang, Andrew, Joseph Chen, and Yuhang Xing, 2006, Downside Risk, *The Review of Financial Studies* 19 (4), 1191–1239.

Baumol, William J., 1963, An Expected Gain-Confidence Limit Criterion for Portfolio Selection, *Management Science* 10, 174–182.

Bawa, Vijay S., and Eric B. Lindenberg, 1977, Capital Market Equilibrium in a Mean-Lower Partial Moment Framework, *Journal of Financial Economics* 5, 189–200.

Black, Fischer, 1972, Capital Market Equilibrium with Restricted Borrowing, *Journal of Business* 45, 444–454.

Blitz, David C., and Jouke Hottinga, 2001, Tracking Error Allocation, *The Journal of Portfolio Management* 27, 19–25.

Brennan, Michael J., 1993, Agency and Asset Pricing, University of California, Los Angeles, working paper.

Brinson, Gary P., L. Randolph Hood, and Gilbert L. Beebower, 1986, Determinants of Portfolio Performance, *Financial Analysts Journal* 42 (4), 39–44.

Brinson, Gary P., Brian D. Singer, and Gilbert L. Beebower, 1991, Determinants of Portfolio Performance II: An Update, *Financial Analysts Journal* 47 (3), 40–48.

Bronstein, Ilja N., Konstantin A. Semendjajew, Gerhard Musiol, and Heiner Mülig, 1997, *Taschenbuch der Mathematik*, Verlag Harri Deutsch, Frankfurt am Main, 3. edition.

Cardon, Pierre, and Joachim Coche, 2004, Strategic Asset Allocation for Foreign Exchange Reserves, In: Bernadell, Carlos, Pierre Cardon, Joachim Coche, Francis X. Diebold, and Simone Manganelli, editors, *Risk Management for Central Bank Foreign Reserves*, 291–304, European Central Bank, Frankfurt am Main.

Carhart, Mark M., 1997, On Persistence in Mutual Fund Performance, *The Journal of Finance* 52 (1), 57–82.

Clarke, Roger G., Harindra de Silva, and Brett Wander, 2002, Risk Allocation versus Asset Allocation, *The Journal of Portfolio Management* 29 (1), 9–30.

Cochrane, John H., 2005, *Asset Pricing*, Princeton University Press, Princeton.

Cornell, Bradford, and Richard Roll, 2005, A Delegated-Agent Asset-Pricing Model, *Financial Analysts Journal* 61, 57–69.

Gómez, Juan-Pedro, and Fernando Zapatero, 2003, Asset Pricing Implications of Benchmarking: A Two-Factor CAPM, *The European Journal of Finance* 9, 343–357.

Harlow, W. V., and Ramesh K. S. Rao, 1989, Asset Pricing in a Generalized Mean-Lower Partial Moment Framework: Theory and Evidence, *The Journal of Financial and Quantitative Analysis* 24 (3), 285–311.

Herold, Ulf, Raimond Maurer, Michael Stamos, and Huy Thanh Vo, 2007, Total Return Strategies for Multi-Asset Portfolios, *The Journal of Portfolio Management* 33 (2), 60–76.

Ho, Clement, 2004, Foreign Reserves Risk Management in Hong Kong, In: Bernadell, Carlos, Pierre Cardon, Joachim Coche, Francis X. Diebold, and Simone Manganelli, editors, *Risk Management for Central Bank Foreign Reserves*, 291–304, European Central Bank, Frankfurt am Main.

Hogan, William W., and James M. Warren, 1974, Toward the Development of an Equilibrium Capital-Market Model Based on Semivariance, *The Journal of Financial and Quantitative Analysis* 9 (1), 1–11.

Ibbotson, Roger G., and Paul D. Kaplan, 2000, Practical Risk Management for Equity Portfolio Managers, *Financial Analysts Journal* 56 (1), 26–33.

Jarre, Florian, and Josef Stoer, 2004, *Optimierung*, Springer, Berlin.

Jensen, Michael C., and William H. Meckling, 1976, Theory of the Firm: Managerial Behavior, Agency Costs and Ownership Structure, *Journal of Financial Economics* 3 (4), 305–360.

Jorion, Philippe, 2003, Portfolio Optimization with Tracking-Error Constraints, *Financial Analysts Journal* 59, 70–82.

Kalin, Dieter, and Rudi Zagst, 1999, Portfolio Constraints: Volatility Constraints Versus Shortfall Constraints, *OR Spektrum* 21, 97–122.

Karush, William, 1939, *Minima of Functions of Several Variables with Inequalities as Side Constraints*, Master of Science Thesis, Department of Mathematics, University of Chicago, Chicago, Illinois.

Kataoka, Shinji, 1963, A Stochastic Programming Model, *Econometrica* 31, 181–196.

Kraft, Holger, and Ralf Korn, 2007, Continuous-time Delegated Portfolio Management with Homogeneous Expectations: Can an Agency Conflict be Avoided?, *Financial Markets and Portfolio Management,* fourthcoming.

Kuhn, Harold W., and Albert W. Tucker, 1950, Nonlinear Programming, In: Neyman, J., editor, *Proceedings of the Second Berkeley Symposium on Mathematical Statistics and Probability*, 481–492, University of California Press, Berkeley.

Lagrange, Joseph-Louis, 1797, *Théorie des fonctions analytiques*, Imprimerie de la Republique, Paris.

Lee, Wai, 2000, *Theory and Methodology of Tactical Asset Allocation*, John Wiley and Sons.

Lee, Wai, and Daniel Y. Lam, 2001, Implementing Optimal Risk Budgeting, *The Journal of Portfolio Management* 28, 73–80.

Lintner, John, 1965, The Valuation of Risk Assets and the Selection of Risky Investment in Stock Portfolios and Capital Budgets, *Review of Economics and Statistics* 47, 13–37.

Malkiel, Burton G., 1995, Returns from Investing in Equity Mutual Funds 1971 to 1991, *The Journal of Finance* 50 (2), 549–572.

Markowitz, Harry, 1952, Portfolio Selection, *Journal of Finance* 7, 77–99.

Merton, Robert C., 1972, An Analytic Derivation of the Efficient Portfolio Frontier, *The Journal of Financial and Quantitative Analysis* 7, 1851–1872.

Mirrlees, James A., 1976, The Optimal Structure of Incentives and Authority within an Organization, *The Bell Journal of Economics* 7 (1), 105–131.

Mirrlees, James A., 1999, The Theory of Moral Hazard and Unobservable Behaviour: Part I., *Review of Economic Studies* 66, 3–21.

Molenkamp, Jan B., 2004, Risk Allocation Under Shortfall Constraints, *The Journal of Portfolio Management* 30 (2), 46–52.

Mossin, Jan, 1966, Equilibrium in a Capital Asset Market, *Econometrica* 34, 768–783.

Reichling, Peter, 1996, Safety First-Ansätze in der Portfolio-Selektion, *Zeitschrift für betriebswirtschaftliche Forschung* 48 (1), 31–55.

Roll, Richard, 1977, A Critique of the Asset Pricing Theorys Tests: Part I: On Past and Potential Testability of the Theory, *Journal of Financial Economics* 4, 129–176.

Roll, Richard, 1980, Orthogonal Portfolios, *Journal of Financial and Quantitative Analysis* 15, 1005–1023.

Roll, Richard, 1992, A Mean/Variance Analysis of Tracking Error, *Journal of Portfolio Management* 18, 13–22.

Ross, Stephen A., 1973, The Economic Theory of Agenncy: The Principal's Problem, *The American Economic Review* 63 (2), 134–139.

Roy, Andrew, 1952, Safety-First and the Holding of Assets, *Econometrica* 20, 431–449.

Scherer, Bernd, 2004, *Portfolio Construction and Risk Budgeting*, Risk Waters Group, London, 2. edition.

Sharpe, William F., 1964, Capital Asset Prices: A Theory of Market Equilibrium Under Conditions of Risk, *Journal of Finance* 19, 425–442.

Sharpe, William F., 1966, Mutual Fund Performance, *The Journal of Business* 39, 119–138.

Sharpe, William F., 2002, Budgeting and Monitoring Pension Fund Risk, *Financial Analysts Journal* 58 (5), 74–86.

Slater, Morton L., 1950, Lagrange Multipliers Revisited: A Contribution to Non-Linear Programming, Cowles Commission Discussion Paper: Mathematics 403.

Starck, Markus O., and Siegfried Trautmann, 2006, Reduktionsmodelle zur Kreditderivatebewertung, In: Kürsten, Wolfgang, and Bernhard Nietert, editors, *Kapitalmarkt, Unternehmensfinanzierung und rationale Entscheidungen*, 473–492, Springer, Heidelberg.

Stein, David M., and Greg McIntire, 2003, Overlay Portfolio Management in a Multi-Manager Account, *Journal of Wealth Management* 5 (4), 57–71.

Stoughton, Neal M., 1993, Moral Hazard and the Portfolio Management Problem, *The Journal of Finance* 48 (5), 2009–2028.

Stracca, Livio, 2005, Delegated Portfolio Management: A Survey of the Theoretical Literature, *Journal of Economic Surveys,* fourthcoming.

Telser, Lester G., 1955, Safety First and Hedging, *Review of Economic Studies* 23, 1–16.

Tobin, James, 1958, Liquidity Preference as Behavior Towards Risk, *Review of Economic Studies* 25, 68–85.

Trautmann, Siegfried, 2007, *Investitionen: Bewertung, Auswahl und Risikomanagement*, Springer, Berlin, 2. edition.

Treynor, Jack L., and Fischer Black, 1973, How to Use Security Analysis to Improve Portfolio Selection, *The Journal of Business* 46, 66–86.

van Binsbergen, Jules H., Michael W. Brandt, and Ralph S. J. Koijen, 2007, Optimal Decentralized Investment Management, *Journal of Finance,* forthcoming.

Waring, Barton, Duane Whitney, John Pirone, and Charles Castille, 2000, Optimizing Manager Structure and Budgeting Manager Risk, *Journal of Portfolio Management* 26 (3), 90–103.

Wermers, Russ, 2000, Mutual Fund Performance: An Empirical Decomposition into Stock-Picking Talent, Style, Transactions Costs, and Expenses, *The Journal of Finance* 55 (4), 1655–1695.

Williamson, Oliver E., 2000, The New Institutional Economics: Taking Stock, Looking Ahead, *Journal of Economic Literature* 38, 595–613.

List of Cited Laws

Gesetz über Kapitalanlagegesellschaften (KAGG), September 9, 1998, in: Bundesgesetzblatt Jahrgang 1998, Teil I Nr. 62, issued on September 17, 1998, Bonn, pp. 2727–2764.

Gesetz zur weiteren Fortentwicklung des Finanzplatzes Deutschland (Viertes Finanzmarktförderungsgesetz), June 21, 2002, in Bundesgesetzblatt Jahrgang 2002, Teil I Nr. 39, issued on Juni 26, 2002, Bonn, pp. 2010–2072.

Gesetz zur Modernisierung des Investmentwesens und zur Besteuerung von Investmentvermögen (Investmentmodernisierungsgesetz), Dezember 15, 2003, in: Bundesgesetzblatt Jahrgang 2003, Teil I Nr. 62, issued on Dezember 19, 2003, Bonn, pp. 2676–2736.

Author Index

General Index

Curriculum Vitae

Personal Data

Name	Markus Otto Starck
Address	Mühlweg 40, 55128 Mainz, Germany
Date and place of birth	November 14, 1975, Germersheim
Marital status	married
Citizenship	German

Education

Aug 1986 – Jun 1995	*Eduard-Spranger-Gymnasium, Landau in der Pfalz* Abitur (Grade: 1.7)
Oct 1996 – Feb 2003	*Universität Karlsruhe (TH)* Studies of Business Mathematics Diploma in Business Mathematics (Grade: "sehr gut")
Sep 1999 – May 2000	*University of Massachusetts at Amherst, United States* Studies of Applied Mathematics Master of Science in Applied Mathematics (GPA: 3.8)

Work Experience

Jul 2000 – Sep 2000	*Arthur Andersen WPG StBG mbH, Eschborn* Internship at the Department Technology Risk Consulting
Oct 2001 – Mar 2007	*Johannes Gutenberg-Universität Mainz,* *CoFaR Center of Finance and Risk Management* Research Assistant supervised by Prof. Dr. S. Trautmann
Nov 2005	*Dongbei University of Finance and Economics, Dalian, China* Visiting Lecturer at the School of International Business